RELATIONAL

ACUITY 2.0

Amplifying Kingdom Etiquette

Tiffany Buckner

Relational Acuity 2.0
Amplifying Kingdom Etiquette

©2022, Tiffany Buckner
www.tiffanybuckner.com
info@tiffanybuckner.com

Published by Anointed Fire House

Edited by:
Anointed Fire House
J. Junga

ISBN: 978-1-955557-25-2

TABLE OF CONTENTS

Introduction

Relational Acuity 2.0: Amplifying Kingdom Etiquette is more than a book of language; it is a book of answers, strategies and instructions. This powerful, refreshing and stimulating guide will help you to better categorize and arrange your relationships, set proper boundaries and peel back the layers of trauma you may have acquired as a result of toxic relationships. The objective is to help you to acquire and amplify the etiquette of God's Kingdom.

Every kingdom has a culture, a language, an accent and a set of rules that governs it, and the Kingdom of God is no different. Surprisingly enough, most Christians are unaware of Kingdom culture, which is why so many of us repeatedly experience the results of the world. This powerful book is designed to address this very matter. Relational Acuity was written for the believer who wants to ascend in the Earth and the Kingdom of God. This amazing, extraordinary and life-altering guide is replete with Kingdom principles and revelation designed to help you grow your relational intelligence. All the same, you will learn how to identify and break relational curses, respond to relational witchcraft and build a world for yourself where the blessings and favor of God are bountiful, a world that is almost impenetrable to the agents of darkness.

Pair this powerful guide with Relational Acuity 1.0 and watch your mind shift so dramatically that your life will never be the same! Additionally, this powerful and brilliant book will help you to better understand how God wired you; this knowledge will help you to better arrange your relationships so that you can maximize the benefits of those relationships, all the while maintaining your sanity! And it goes without saying that Relational Acuity will help you to grow in the areas of relational and emotional intelligence, thus setting the stage for the blessings of God to freely flow in your life.

Levels of the Heart

As a refresher from Relational Acuity 1.0, there are five access points to the heart. They are Circles 1-5. Let's look at each definition again, followed by a chart. The following info was taken from Relational Acuity 1.0:

1. **Circle 5** is your communal space; this is an intellectual zone or space. This is where you meet people. It represents the most distant form of intellectual access; this means that the person has a measure of personal access to you, but the two of you don't really know one another. This is where you meet; this is where you commune. If the person is decent, you'd likely invite him or her into Circle 4.

2. **Circle 4** is your phone number. Now, just because someone has your phone number doesn't automatically mean that the person is in Circle 4. Your phone number is simply an invitation to this circle IF you have been communicating with the person in the communal space that you two share, and if you've shared a certain amount of intimate information and vice versa. If you have never communicated with the person, on the other hand, and the individual asks for your phone number, the person will enter into Circle 5 when he or she calls you. Circle 4 is your way of giving a person permission to be in constant contact with you, whether this frequency looks like a month, a few months, weeks or days.

3. **Circle 3** is your living room. This space can be both intimate and intellectual. For example, you may open the door for a neighbor you don't personally know if she asks to borrow something from you. By allowing her into your home, you are expressing a certain level of trust, but chances are, you wouldn't invite her to take a seat or ask if she wants something to drink.

4. **Circle 2** is your kitchen. While this is an intimate space, you would likely invite people into this space that you trust and have built a measure of rapport with.

5. **Circle 1** is your bedroom. This is the most intimate space in the house, only reserved for people who have the most intimate connection with you; this includes your spouse, your parents and your closest friends.

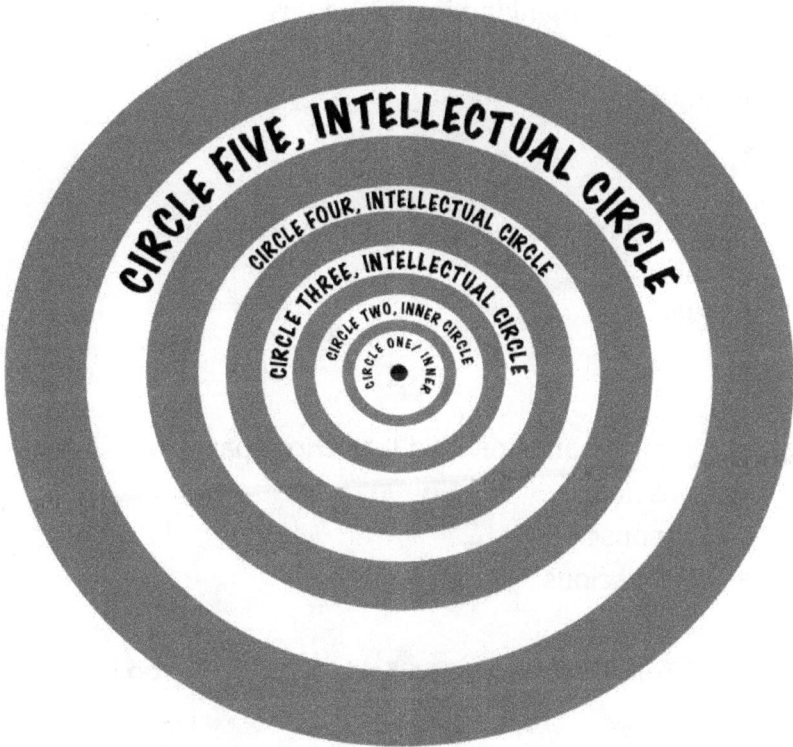

In 1.0, we discussed the many states of the human heart. Before we go any further, let's look at two scriptures:

- **1 Corinthians 6:17**: But he that is joined unto the Lord is one spirit.
- **Genesis 2:24**: Therefore shall a man leave his father and his mother, and shall cleave unto his wife: and they shall be one flesh.

So, we become one flesh with our spouses when we join ourselves to them, just as we become one spirit with God when we join ourselves to Him. Both unions are referred to as marriages. Merriam Webster defines the word "marriage" this way: "an intimate or close union."

3

Remember that mankind is divided into three parts:
- Body
- Soul
- Spirit

The soul of a man is divided into three parts:
- Mind
- Will
- Emotions

The mind of a man is divided into three parts:
- Conscious
- Subconscious
- Unconscious

30 Fold	60 Fold	100 Fold
Conscious	Subconscious	Unconscious
Outer Court	Inner Court	Holy of Holies

Every person that you meet will first enter the outer court of your soul. This doesn't mean that they will be physically there; it means that you will allow them a measure of access to your heart. Let's visit the world of psychology to get a better understanding of this. The following information was taken from Medium.com, a website for writers. Anyhow, here's (part of) the article:

> "The conscious mind consists of what we are aware of at any given point in time. It includes the things that we are thinking about right now, whether it's in the front of our minds or the back. If we're aware of

it, then it is in the conscious mind. For example, at this moment you may be consciously aware of the information you're reading, the sound of the music you're listening to, or a conversation you're having. All of the thoughts that pass through your mind, the sensations and perceptions from the outside world, and the memories that you bring into your awareness are all part of that conscious experience. The next level of consciousness, the subconscious (or preconscious), is the stuff from which dreams are made. We can consider it as the storehouse of all remembered experiences, impressions that are left on the mind by such experiences, and tendencies that are awakened or reinforced by these impressions.

Every experience you've ever had, every thought and every impression lives in the subconscious mind and influences our patterns of thought and behavior far more than we realize.

The subconscious holds information that is just below the surface of awareness. An individual can retrieve such information with relative ease, and we usually refer to these as memories.

The final level of consciousness is known as the unconscious. This is made up of thoughts, memories, and primitive/instinctual desires that are buried deep within ourselves, far below our conscious awareness. Even though we're not aware of their existence, they have a significant influence on our behavior.

Although our behaviors tend to indicate the unconscious forces driving them, we can't readily access the information which is stored in the unconscious mind. Throughout our childhood, we gathered many different memories and experiences that formed the beliefs, fears and insecurities that we carry today. However, we cannot recall most of these memories. They are unconscious forces that drive our behaviors" (Source: Medium.com/The Three Levels of Human Consciousness/Kain Ramsay).

Before we go any further, let's address the elephant in the room—science is not an enemy of God, nor does it oppose the Word of God. There are some scientists who oppose the Word, but true science actually confirms the Word. The reason I share this is because some people are bound by the spirit of religion and anytime they see anything dealing with science, they become offended and shut down. This is a form of religious trauma.

Let's talk about romantic relationships. We'll create two characters: Jada and Steven. The couple met at an ice-skating rink and they've been almost inseparable ever since. But before we can discuss their relationship, let's look at Steven's past. His father was a narcissist; his mother idolized men. Steven's father and mother have never officially dated. Instead, they had a sexual relationship 27 years ago, and this is how Steven came to be. Also note that Steven's father has always been an absent father, only resurfacing whenever he wanted to have a series of sexual encounters with Steven's mother. He would always pop up, love-bomb his ex and start showing interest in Steven. But after about a month or two, he would always get bored and disappear all over again. When Steven turned 12-years old, this behavior ceased because Steven confronted his father one summer when he'd attempted to reemerge. All the same, to ensure that his father would not come back, Steven told his father about his mother's out-of-state boyfriend. "Jason was over here last week trying to be my father! Please go away. I can only handle one father at a time," he'd said, completely humillating his mother and infuriating his father. And since then, Steven has not heard from his father. Where is Steven wounded? In the paternal state, of course. And his wounds extend outside of the "father room," they are also found in the "mother room." This is because Steven has had to see his mother going from one relationship to the next all of his life. Consequently, he would emotionally attach himself to some of his mother's lovers, only to have them disappear without a trace. This caused a great deal of confusion and rejection in his young life. To add insult to injury, Steven's mother would often leave him home alone with his younger siblings whenever she couldn't find a babysitter. And she didn't care who babysat her children. She was always looking for an opportunity to get out of the house to party. Her children, to her, were nothing but burdens or rejected sacrificial offerings. And when Steven turned 18-years old, his mother put him out of her house simply because her new boyfriend had been complaining about him defending himself whenever he berated him. With nowhere to turn,

Steven went to live in a shelter. After he left the shelter, he moved in with an old friend of his. The two guys were inseparable; they were so close that people would remark about how close in resemblance they were. His friend, Jordan, worked at a car dealership, and he would often be gone for the majority of the day on most days.

Two months into living with Jordan, Steven met a young woman named Star. Star was beautiful to look upon and neatly shaped. Her shoulder-length hair was always curly. It always looked like she'd just gotten out of the shower. And Steven was smitten with this young beauty. Things were looking up for the Steven. He ended up landing a job at a local supermarket, plus, he'd gotten accepted to an accredited university. Whenever he wasn't at work, Steven spent every waking moment with Star, so when she announced that she was pregnant, he was besides himself with excitement. She was nothing like the other women from his past who'd hurt or rejected him. Star was confident and nurturing. She was everything Steven wanted in a woman and more.

One day, Steven went to work, only to find that his work identification number did not work. He went to the human resources department to find out what had gone wrong. This is when he discovered that he'd gotten his third strike yesterday because he had been marked as a no-call, no show. He went to the manager's office and tried to explain to the manager that he had been marked as off. To this, the manager replied that the schedule had been changed a few days ago, and it is the responsibility of every employee to keep watch of the schedule. His first two strikes had been from customer complaints. One woman had complained two months earlier that he'd ignored her when she'd asked for help, and while this wasn't true, his manager had taken her word over Steven's. Another complaint had come from a former employee who'd come to the store to shop. He'd claimed that Steven had refused to help him because he'd come to the store shopping with one of Steven's ex-girlfriends, and while this was true, Steven reasoned that he would be avoiding unnecessary drama by refusing to help the couple. After all, that particular ex-girlfriend had not only cheated on him with his brother, she'd gone out of her way to sabotage his life simply because he'd ended his relationship with her. He knew that her interest in his former co-worker had everything to do with her hatred for him. Nevertheless, this had been logged as a pink slip, and consequently, it had put a mark on his file. And now, there he was standing in the manager's office, being told that he was no longer an employee. Hurt and disgusted, Steven left the store promising himself that he'd have another job by the end of the week so he could be sure to help his dear friend out on the bills. He called Jordan to tell him the bad news and ask him if he'd be willing to pick him up from work, but he didn't get an answer.

Twenty minutes later, Steven managed to secure himself a taxi. And thirty minutes later, he pulled up in front of his home. Jordan's car was in the driveway. This was relatively odd considering the fact that Steven had called him, but he hadn't answered his phone. Nevertheless, Steven reasoned in his heart that maybe Jordan was asleep. Steven walked up to the door and unlocked it with his key. Something felt off. Something felt odd or out of place. What was he about to witness? "Why does this feel like a crime scene?" Steven thought to himself. "I hope I don't come across a dead body." Seconds later, Steven wrapped his hand around the doorknob to his bedroom. What he found on the other side of the door was horrific! There lie Jordan and Steven's new girlfriend, Star. They were partially clothed and sound asleep. Star opened her eyes first and let out a guttural scream. This scared Jordan out of his sleep. He immediately jumped from the bed and threw his hands up defensively. "Get out of my house," he shouted at Steven. Of course, Steven was shocked. "Get out before I call the cops!" Steven didn't say a word. Once again, his heart had been crushed. He left Jordan's house without taking a single item of clothing with him. He reasoned that he wouldn't need any of his belongings for where he was about to go. He planned to commit suicide, but these plans had been thwarted when he'd remembered that Star was pregnant. "I'm taking custody of my child," he reasoned with himself. "I'm going to get my life together so I can give my child a better life than the one I've had!"

Six months later, Steven was excited to hear that Star had just given birth to a healthy baby boy. By this time, he had an amazing job with the post office and he had his own apartment, plus, he was about to finish his first semester at school. It goes without saying that he was devastated to discover that the boy Star had given birth to was not his son. His former friend, Jordan, was even more stunned to discover that the child wasn't his either. Nevertheless, Steven decided to move on with his life, reasoning within himself that someday, everyone who had ever hurt him would regret doing so. Four months after this, he met Jada at an ice-skating rink. Jada was a beautiful, God-fearing young woman who always seemed to be excited about something. Her over-the-top personality and infectious smile had Steven completely smitten, and Jada was smitten with him as well. The two made a beautiful couple, but their romance would be challenged by the demons from Steven's past.

It all started one day when Jada had fallen asleep midday. Consequently, she'd missed several of Steven's calls. Now, Jada was a faithful young woman who hoped to someday meet and marry a man who loved the Lord ... a man who would love her, cherish her and remain faithful to her. And she understood that to attract this type of guy, she had to be this type of woman, and Steven appeared to be the right guy for the job! But on this day, a dark side of Steven emerged. He'd left her two very unsettling voice messages, one in which he'd threatened to kill her and then kill himself. Jada couldn't believe what she was hearing. How could such a loving, humble and kind guy turn into such a monster? With thirteen missed calls, two voice messages and four ugly text messages, Jada decided to drive over to Steven's apartment. When she arrived, she found Steven outside calling her phone yet again. He was pacing back and forth, and he didn't look like his usual self. He looked like a crazed maniac. Jada wondered whether or not it would be a great idea to approach Steven, but after he'd spotted her in the car, she decided to get out. The couple argued, Jada broke up with Steven and then, he apologized. Steven begged his now ex-girlfriend for her forgiveness. "I'm sorry. I got scared!" he shouted. "I love you, Jada! And that scares me!" Jada knew Steven's story, so she had compassion for him. "Let's go inside," she said, wiping a lone tear away from his face.

Once inside, the couple sat down and Jada began to speak. "I am not Star," she said. "I have never cheated on you and I would never cheat on you. Steven, I love you despite how crazy you clearly are. I need you to trust me because today, you truly scared me!" Steven agreed. "I promise I'll never behave like this again. You have my word, baby! Just please don't ever leave me. I need you, Jada! I need you!" With these words, Steven laid his head on Jada's lap and began to weep. She caressed his hair, rocked gently and sang his favorite song to him. What Jada didn't know was that Steven was not well. Sure, he had the potential to become an amazing husband, but the truth of the matter was that he was a wounded soul and he'd never done anything to heal from his past traumas. Let's imagine that Steven had five levels to his heart, and the only woman who'd ever occupied Level One had been his mother. Of course, she'd damaged him majorly, so he unconsciously made that level off limits to every person. Nevertheless, he'd allowed one of his exes into Level Two and she'd damaged him like no other woman. That's when he met Star. Star had occupied Level Three and she was well on her way to moving up a level before he'd discovered her indiscretions. Each woman had been a hand grenade of sorts, causing utter chaos in every level of his heart. Consequently, because of his traumas, Steven had always kept every other woman in the fourth level. Any time a woman was on the verge of graduating from this level, he'd sabotage the relationship. And now, Jada sat there rocking and comforting him, not realizing that she'd just graduated to Level Three. This sounds great and grand, but you have to understand that Steven's heart is in ruins; this causes him to be insecure and distrusting.

After this, Steven tries a few times to sabotage the relationship, but to no avail. Jada fights for their relationship because she is determined to prove to her lover that she is nothing like the women from his past. What she doesn't realize is that she is descending into the darkness of his heart. Imagine it this way. Steven's heart is void; it is absent of light (revelation). His heart represents Level One. Level Five, on the other hand, was completely bright or brilliant because he still had hope. Hope can be built on the right foundation or the wrong one. In Steven's case, his hope had been built on the belief that some woman would come along, and that woman would heal his wounds, make his life better and help him to navigate through this event we so passionately refer to as life. In other words, he was looking for a woman to fill a God-sized void in his heart, and we all know how stories like these end! This means that his hope would repeatedly be deferred which, in turn, would make his heart sick (see Proverbs 13:12). Now imagine the other levels; they should look like a gradient between light and darkness (see image).

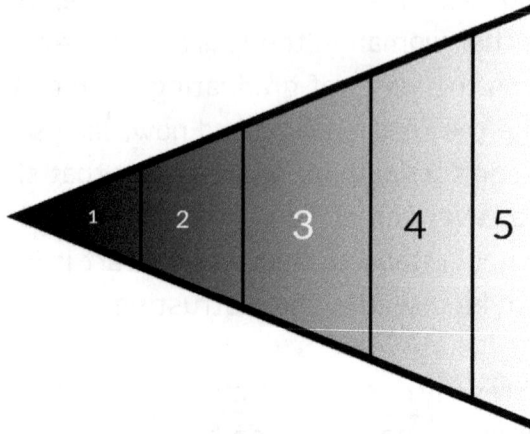

In the beginning of every relationship, Steven is an amazing boyfriend! He's hopeful, positive and considerate! But any woman who dared to ascend the ranks of Steven's heart, unbeknownst to her, was slowly walking towards the darkness. After all, the closer or more intimate she got with Steven, the darker he appeared to be. This is because Steven feared allowing anyone to occupy that particular space in his heart because he did not want to experience the pain of a breakup or the pangs of betrayal. All the same, he didn't trust himself with that type of pain. So, he guarded his heart, but not in a Godly way. Steven used the spirit of sabotage to guard his heart. He partnered with the Leviathan spirit to keep his relationships at surface-level. But again, Jada managed to slip past all of his fears and insecurities until she found herself in Level Three. Remember:

1. You should NEVER arrive in a place or dimension of a person's soul before God is invited into that space.
2. When you occupy a space before God occupies that space, you will become an idol; this will undoubtedly place you in danger.
3. Demons live in voids (darkness).

When Jada entered Level Three, Steven reasoned within himself that he could not live without her, so he went and bought an engagement ring. The two were engaged, and five months later, they got married. This would be the beginning of Jada's woes. Sure, we'd love to believe Hollywood's depiction of love, but that's not realistic. True love can never be separate from God. Remember this—God is love, so when someone says "I love you," that person is saying, "I have God's heart for you." If he (or she) doesn't have God's heart, how can he (or she) have God's heart for you? Jesus said, in Luke 10:27, that we are to love the Lord with all our hearts, with all our souls, with all our strength, and with all our minds. After this, our assignment was to love ourselves, and then share this love with our neighbors.

Steven didn't love Jada because he had not yet learned to love the Lord, and this was evidenced in the fact that he had trouble loving himself. So, while Jada is a decent and honorable woman, Steven lives in the past. It goes without saying that he will break her time and time again until she decides to get up and leave or she becomes a shell of a woman. Sadly enough, the moment Jada decides to distance herself from Steven, he will likely consider taking her life.

God has to enter into the innermost chambers of our hearts before we are considered healthy enough to have intimate relationships with others. This means that we need to spend intimate time with God so that He can fill our innermost being; the same is true for the people we choose to bring close to us. Understand that not everyone can have intimate access to you, after all, your heart is sacred. This is why Satan passionately wants to invade it. Delilah had intimate access to Samson's heart, and we all know how that went.

Patterns and Principles

God designed us all in a unique way. You are the only version of yourself who has ever existed and who will ever exist. You are one of a kind, even though there are people out there who share some of the same graces, anointing, characteristics and proclivities that you get to enjoy. Nevertheless, there has never been and never will be a person (outside of Christ) who embodies the totality of who you are. I suspect that many people will stand before Christ someday, and as they are being introduced to Him, they will be introduced to themselves. It is in that hour that they will realize just how much potential or untapped power they once had when they'd lived on Earth. They will see themselves as the kings and queens they are. Howbeit, in that moment, there will be no do-overs or excuses; instead, many will be like the unfaithful servant. Matthew 25:14-30 tells the story. It reads, "For the kingdom of heaven is as a man traveling into a far country, who called his own servants, and delivered unto them his goods. And unto one he gave five talents, to another two, and to another one; to every man according to his several ability; and straightway took his journey. Then he that had received the five talents went and traded with the same, and made them other five talents. And likewise he that had received two, he also gained other two. But he that had received one went and digged in the earth, and hid his lord's money. After a long time the lord of those servants cometh, and reckoneth with them. And so he that had received five talents came and brought other five talents, saying, Lord, thou deliveredst unto me five talents: behold, I have gained beside them five talents more. His lord said unto him, Well done, thou good and faithful servant: thou hast been faithful over a few things, I will make thee ruler over many things: enter thou into the joy of thy lord. He also that had received two talents came and said, Lord, thou deliveredst unto me two talents: behold, I have gained two other talents beside them. His lord said unto him, Well done, good and faithful servant; thou hast been faithful over a few things, I will make thee ruler over many things: enter thou into the joy of thy lord. Then he which had received the one talent came and said, Lord, I knew thee that thou art an hard man, reaping where thou hast not sown, and gathering where thou hast not strawed: And I was afraid, and went and hid thy talent in the earth: lo, there thou hast that is thine. His lord answered and said unto him, Thou wicked and slothful servant, thou knewest that I reap where I sowed not, and gather where I have not strawed: Thou oughtest therefore to have put my money to the exchangers, and then at my coming I should have received mine own with usury. Take therefore the talent from him, and give it unto him which hath ten talents. For unto every one that hath shall be given, and he shall have abundance: but from him that hath not shall be taken away even that which he hath. And cast ye the unprofitable servant into outer darkness: there shall be weeping and gnashing of teeth."

Notice that the unfaithful servant had convinced himself that his master was an evil man, and because of how he viewed his master, he feared and despised him. This is what religion does. It causes those who adhere to it to have what we in the church call a "works mentality." Simply put, a works mentality looks like this:

1. The individual submitted to it fears hell, not God.
2. The individual submitted to it envisions God to be a taskmaster who is angry with him or her, and overly determined to send the individual to hell.
3. The person submitted to it performs a lot of religious works and ritualistic acts in an attempt to pacify God's wrath.
4. Under the law, there is and was no casting out of demons, therefore, the person submitted to religion will repeatedly fail at doing the right thing because of the strongholds in his or her life. All the same, the individual will likely be in need of deliverance, but won't get it. So, the person submitted to it will become frustrated and begin to despise God, all the while performing for Him in an attempt to be accepted into Heaven.
5. The person submitted to it will not bear any Godly fruits, but will instead repeatedly reap sorrow.

Faith is an opponent of fear and fear is the enemy of faith. When we stand before God, our faith will testify on our behalf or the spirit of fear will accuse us before the Lord. Simply put, the unfaithful servant did not wholeheartedly know his master, and because he didn't know him, he didn't trust him, nor did he love him. This is why 1 John 4:18 says, "There is no fear in love; but perfect love casteth out fear: because fear hath torment. He that feareth is not made perfect in love." The words "perfect love" can be translated as "ripe love" or "mature love." This indicates that there are stages of love, with the highest level being "perfect love." What I've discovered on my journey in love is this—you cannot love what or who you do not know. This means that we cannot love YAHWEH if we do not know Him. And we cannot know Him if we do not pursue Him through Bible study, prayer and worship. All the same, trust is not built merely through us exegeting the scriptures. Trust is built through the application of God's Word. This is why the Bible tells us that faith without works is dead. The works that we do reveal our hearts and establishes our patterns. It also aids us in understanding the patterns of God. This isn't to say that God is predictable, after all, He uses the foolish things of this world to confound the wise. It is to say, however, that God has habits. Habits are what creates habitats or dwelling places. God is good; He is faithful, holy, beautiful and true, and He is this way consistently. Therefore, He can only inhabit spaces that are good, faith-filled, holy, beautiful and established in truth. This is why we have to create an environment through prayer and worship to host God's presence. Additionally, God has principles, and those principles are executed or carried out by a group of spirits called principalities. Please note that there are both good and evil principalities. Principalities are angelic hosts who guard and sustain a set of principles in a family, a community, a region, a country, a religion or an organization; they are the governing agents of systems. And lastly, please note that every pattern is founded on a set of principles, and every principle is fueled by patterns.

You're wired to perform a certain set of functions. For example, if you are a prophet, you are wired to prophesy. And, of course, the world of the prophetic isn't just limited to words. People prophesy through the many arts, including (but not limited to) dancing, painting, singing, acting, writing, etc. Think of Joseph's coat of many colors. It wasn't just a coat; it was a piece of fabric that had been knit together prophetically to represent the many worlds that Joseph would go into. Of course, Joseph's father, Jacob, didn't know this when he was making the coat. Like most prophets and prophetic people, he simply felt inspired to create.

Again, if you are a prophet or a prophetic person, you are wired to prophesy in one way or another. You're also wired to be relatively sensitive. This sensitivity was designed so that you could easily sense the presence of the Lord. It also helps you to discern unclean spirits. Howbeit, before you knew who you were, the enemy noticed your wiring and decided to pervert your patterns by hijacking your wiring. Another way of saying this is—he caught you when you were young and easily influenced, and he threw a lot of darts at you. His objective was to get you entangled in a lot of ungodly and unhealthy behaviors, and then repeatedly lure you back into those behaviors until they became habits. After this, you'd create a habitat to host those behaviors. This habitat is called a stronghold. You see, trauma causes people to go into survival mode. If they don't get the information they need to come out of that region of thought, they will make it their dwelling place by establishing a bunch of ungodly and unhealthy patterns of behavior. These habits, once solidified, become what we refer to as "strongholds." Oxford Languages' online dictionary defines the word "stronghold" as "a place where a particular cause or belief is strongly defended or upheld." Notice here that a stronghold is NOT a set of beliefs, but is instead "a place" where a particular set of beliefs are upheld. I immediately think about some of the areas I lived in while I was growing up. There were dominant beliefs in those areas, just as there were passive beliefs. One belief that is upheld in many urban and rural areas is the "no snitch" rule. This simply means that if a person sees a crime being committed or knows someone who has committed a crime, no matter how heinous the crime is, the individual must pretend to know nothing. People who freely speak with law enforcement in those areas are referred to as "snitches," and they are oftentimes silenced by threats of bodily harm or death. Some people are even assaulted and/or killed. This keeps the people that live in or frequent those areas to adopt those beliefs or, at minimum, the practices, and this is what sustains their habitats. This is an example of a stronghold. Why am I sharing this?

1. You need to pay attention to the strongholds in your life, after all, they are nothing but patterns that have been solidified through repetition.
2. You need to pay attention to the strongholds in the lives of those in your circle or the people who audition for roles in your life.

For example, I used to live on a street (we'll call it Sumter Street) when I was in my mid-twenties. Sumter Street had what we referred to as a rich end, a middle-class end and a ghetto. They were all divided by highways. On one side of the highway was the "good end" as the locals called it. On the other side of the highway was the middle-class end (this is where I lived), and on the other side of the highway was the wealthy end. It was hard to believe that every one of those neighborhoods shared one street, so whenever someone said they lived on Sumter Street, they would always indicate which end they lived on. In short, the middle of Sumter Street was almost like a gradient; the closer you got to the seedy side, the cheaper the houses were. The closer you got to the rich end, the higher the prices were. But it hadn't always been like that! The bad end of Sumter had once housed the wealthy. I'm not sure what happened, but over the course of time, it declined until it became a bad neighborhood. And the locals pretty much understood that the middle end would someday become crime-ridden, while the rich end would one day be considered a middle-class neighborhood. This is because the atmosphere your neighbor creates will align or war with your atmosphere until one of them becomes the principle or dominant habitat for that neighborhood. Think of it this way—have you ever lived in a pretty decent neighborhood, only to have a new neighbor move into that neighborhood and start creating problems? For instance, your new neighbors may blast their music, fight outside, park across their lawns, park in front of your house, have a bunch of questionable folks hanging out at their houses, etc. If so, what you experienced was a person or a group of people trying to set the stage for the principality that governs them by introducing their principles to their new neighborhood. Another way to say this is—the people in question are trying to establish a habitat similar to the one they are accustomed to. If you were bold, you confronted them about some of their behaviors. If you hated confrontation, chances are, you started looking for another home. Either way, there was a war of principles taking place, and if no one fought to maintain the integrity of the neighborhood, it slowly began to spiral downward (morally and spiritually) until the Godly principality (angel) that sat over it was dethroned and replaced by an ungodly principality (demon). I'm sharing this to make a point—this is what happens when you hang around morally bankrupt people OR folks who hang around immoral people.

Remember, in Relational Acuity 1.0, we discussed this fact —you are a word of God, just as Jesus is the Word of God, and everyone you connect to is a word. They are either words of God or they are profane words. Every time you connect with someone, you create a statement. You not only create a statement through them, but through the people they connect themselves to as well. Think about it this way—the men who authored the Bible all had their own unique experiences, and many of their lives and exploits are published for us to read today. Howbeit, their stories are not absent of people. Their stories shed light on how they responded to people and the many obstacles that Satan placed in front of them through those people.

Believe it or not, you are creating a book of your own; this is the account that you will give when you stand before the Lord. And your book won't just be a bunch of stories about you; it will be comprised of your encounters with other people. For example, let's create a character named

Mitchell. Mitchell heads to the gas station one day, and while there, he sees a man standing in front of an old station wagon. The man is parked next to a gas pump just a few feet away from Mitchell's gas pump. Mitchell has just gotten his paycheck, and to his surprise, his paycheck is much higher than it normally is because Mitchell's boss decided to reward him for earning the highest amount of sales in his department. Excited, Mitchell decided to take his new bride to a water park, but on their way there, he came across the man in the station wagon. This guy's name is Earl. Earl is in a dark place in his life. Widowed, homeless and unemployed, Earl decided to risk running out of gas to come to the gas station. His plan was to ask a few people to help him gas up his vehicle so that he could return to Detroit where the rest of his family was. He'd been parked at the pump for more than an hour when Mitchell pulled up. Mitchell was his last hope. The gas station's attendant had come outside three times to tell Earl to leave and, of course, no one had been willing to help the elderly veteran out. But when Earl saw Mitchell pulling into the station, he decided to try one more time. After all, the attendant was now in the station calling the cops and Mitchell was Earl's last hope. The plate on the front of Mitchell's car read "Jesus is Love" and right next to those words was a picture of the American flag, so Earl reasoned with himself that the man pulling up was definitely Christian and maybe even patriotic. Earl walks over to Mitchell as he begins to pump his gas. "Excuse me, sir," he said with his voice quivering. "My name is Earl and I'm a veteran of the United States Army. Sir, please, I need to return to Detroit; that's where my daughter lives. I'm homeless, I can't work and I don't have anything to eat. My daughter is a pregnant single woman, so I can't ask her to travel all this way. Can you spare a few bucks to help me out?" Mitchell becomes annoyed. In short, he refuses to help the elderly man. Consequently, Earl got in his car, drove it until it ran out of gas and the brokenhearted vet froze to death on the side of a highway. Know this— Mitchell will have a chapter in his book called "Earl," and in this chapter, he will see himself as God saw him: greedy, unloving, prideful and hateful. The point I'm making is that everyone you influence in one way or another will have a chapter in your book, just as the people who influence you will have a chapter.

Who do you have in your intimate circle? Who's in your intellectual circle? What stories are you all writing together? Is your book child-friendly or should it be child-proof? You have a region of thought, and the same is true for the people around you. Their regions of thought directly impact the way that you think. And just like Sumter Street, if you have people who lack integrity around you, your integrity will slowly find its way in the slums. This is why 1 Corinthians 15:33 says, "Be not deceived: evil communications corrupt good manners." Look at your patterns, and then look at the patterns of the people around you. This will help you to better understand your habitat or, better yet, what you've reaped thus far on the Earth. If you want to reap better results, you have to build better habits and encourage your friends to do the same. And you have to be willing to put space, time and distance between yourself and the ones who insist on remaining in the ditches of morality. Remember, we are never truly loyal to people; we are loyal to seasons and systems or, better yet, regions of thoughts, and every region of thought is established by a group of principles.

The better way to sum this up is this—imagine the people in your circle as streets. Are they good neighborhoods or bad ones? Do you want your life to look like theirs? If so, bring them closer. If not, place them in your intellectual circle and let them fizzle out of it if they choose to remain in the regions of thought that they're in. If you have to keep them around, place the right labels on your relationships with them. For example, you may be their mentor or their big sister/brother in the Lord. This means that your job is to pour into them whenever the occasion presents itself, to pray with them, to pray for them and to encourage them whenever they need encouragement. Howbeit, do not forget to establish boundaries! After all, some people play the damsel in distress with the sole intent of creating soul ties with the people they want to be connected to, and their desire to connect is sometimes motivated by selfish ambition or need. All the same, their desires to get closer to you can be demonically motivated. For example, over the course of time, you will have people who rush to get close to you, and the moment they feel that you're soul-tied to them, they will start trying to control you. How this looks is—they will try to find a way to secure a spot in your life, and when they feel like they've succeeded in doing so, they'll start threatening you with their absence (if allowed). This is, of course, after they believe they've built value in your life. This is a form of relational witchcraft, and sadly enough, it is pretty commonplace today. How do you respond to relational witchcraft? Communicate your boundaries with them (this is the first warning). And whenever they attempt to control you again, firmly remind them of your boundaries, but this time, start moving them into your intellectual circle, further and further away from your heart. If they violate your boundaries again, cut all ties with them. (Note: in some cases, I've immediately cut ties with toxic people, and in some instances, I've used the grey rock method). What is the grey rock method? Check out the following information below.

"The grey rock method involves communicating in an uninteresting way when interacting with abusive or manipulative people. The name "grey rock" refers to how those using this approach become unresponsive, similar to a rock.
The technique may involve:
- avoiding interactions with the abusive person
- keeping unavoidable interactions brief
- giving short or one-word answers to questions
- communicating in a factual, unemotional way

The aim is to cause the abusive person to lose interest and stop their antagonistic behavior, to protect a person's emotional well-being" (Source: MedicalNewsToday/What is the Grey Rock Method?)

Please note that the grey rock method should NOT be used as a tool of manipulation; it is not designed to bring a narcissist under your control. This method should only be used in relationships with people who you cannot distance yourself from (ex: exes you share a child with, co-workers, roommates, etc.). I always warn people this way—never try to play in a crazy man's head. What this means is don't try to play mind games with a mentally unstable person.

The short of it is this—let your life make a statement through the good patterns that you've established and surround yourself with people who also have good habits. This is how you create your own version of Heaven on Earth. This is how you create Godly systems and processes that will produce good fruits which, in turn, will lead to a good life. Your patterns matter, and so do your principles. Align your heart with God's heart so that His will can be produced (through you) in the Earth.

DIRECTIONAL AND POSITIONAL ACUITY

Imagine yourself as a rotating rack in a store. On one side, there is wisdom, knowledge, discernment and understanding; this is your spiritual side. When a person spins you around, that person will find your comedic side. When that person spins you again, he or she will find your relational (romantic, platonic, familial) side. And when that person spins you again, he or she will find your not-so-pleasant side. Always pay attention to the side of you that every person in your life and every person who attempts to enter into your life tends to pull on. This will tell you a lot about that person, and it will help you to understand the best placement of that person in your life. For example, I have had people who referred to me as their friend, but they spent the majority of their time offended with me about something I said. Don't get me wrong. I didn't say anything offensive. They were just easily offended, and they didn't know how to have relationships with people who didn't fully agree with them. I tell people this all the time—do not surround yourself with people who agree with you, people who are too afraid to disagree with you or people who are on your level. We need people who are smarter than us; these relationships force us to listen more than we speak. They also keep us humble. We need people who have not yet reached our height as it relates to mental or spiritual things; these relationships allow us to pour into others so that everything we've learned is not lost upon ourselves. And lastly, we need eye-level relationships. These are the relationships that we have with people who are equal to us in knowledge and/or rank. All of these relationships are important. They allow us to be the multidimensional, multifaceted and multi-gifted creatures that we were designed to be, but unfortunately, most people limit themselves to a few eye-level relationships and a bunch of relationships where they are required to pour, but they are not being poured into. This is where we get the concept of the "strong friend." In many cases, the strong friend is a victim of his or her own fear of high-level relationships. By this, I mean having people in their lives that outrank them. This is oftentimes a response to chaotic and traumatic childhoods, where the authority figures in their lives mishandled, neglected and/or abused them. Consequently, many of them have a fear of or a disdain for authority figures. They feel safer in relationships where they are needed, but in relationships where they are not needed, they feel insecure. How do I know this? Because I've often been the strong friend. I had to come to terms with the fact that while I love, honor and respect people in authority, I have avoided them a lot in life. That was until the Lord started putting pressure on me to seek wise counsel. I had to intentionally seek and submit to authority figures so that I could be developed properly in that area. Thinking back to my childhood, I can now understand why I felt so insecure around people in authority. I had been abused by a lot of authority figures in my life. Another symptom of a fear of authority is the concept of "loving hard." We don't love hard; we just love improperly. This overcompensation is oftentimes a person's attempt to "make up the difference" or "fill the gap" that they feel was created by what they perceive to be their inferiority. A better way to explain this is—some people may feel like you are far more valuable than they are, and because of this, they feel like they owe you their loyalty for simply doing or saying something nice to them. And if allowed, some of them will put you before God. You should never allow this! Your assignment is to always point them to God! And if you happen to be one of these people, you should definitely consider therapy to help heal and mature you in the areas you feel that you are deficient in. Additionally, be prayerful about everyone who enters or auditions for a role in your life. If someone takes advantage of your insecurities, disconnect from that person. Again, pay attention to what side of you every person seems to be most attracted to. It's great to have sectional or directional relationships, but if someone repeatedly pulls on your carnality, that person shouldn't be in your intimate circle.

Have you ever had a friend, family member or co-worker that you could talk to for days about a specific topic, but whenever you attempted to talk to that person about another topic, the two of you couldn't seem to agree? As a matter of fact, you likely discovered that you could only discuss one or a few subjects with the person, but every other subject was off limits. If this has happened to you, you've experienced what I call a directional affiliate. What is a directional affiliate? This is a person who is or can be your friend in one area, but an enemy or a stranger in another area. A good example is the ever-so-popular topic of politics. Let's say that you are a Republican, but your good friend, Bob, is a Democrat. You and Bob met 18 years ago at a golf resort, and the two of you bonded over your passion for golf, your love of family and your Christian faith. Nevertheless, the one topic that divides the two of you is politics. Both you and Bob vehemently oppose public assistance, but for different reasons. You want public assistance cut down by eighty percent, with the remaining twenty percent being given to the elderly and the handicapped. Bob, on the other hand, thinks that the public assistance model should simply be reformed. According to Bob, cutting off public assistance would severely cripple our country, so he proposes that the funds be allocated to companies, thus giving them more money to hire people. And anyone who applies for public assistance would be required to work at one of those places. Both of you make good points, but no matter how much you try to reason together, you're both too passionate about your views. This means that Bob is your political enemy, even though you consider him a friend in every other area. One of the lessons that most of us have never been taught is this— you can have directional relationships with people. Think about a married couple. It is not uncommon to see an introverted man married to an extroverted woman. This is where the old saying "opposites attract" comes from. Howbeit, for whatever reason, many people have missed out on, spoiled and even sabotaged some pretty valuable relationships simply because they found an area that they did not agree in. We see it all the time—someone you know calls your phone and starts a conversation about anything from the weather to the price of gasoline. This is a person who doesn't call you often, so you know that there's something else the individual wants to talk to you about (let's pretend this person is a woman named Raven to make this flow better). Finally, Raven finds a way to bring up one of her close friends' names. "I'm not gossiping about her," she says. "After all, she is my friend, but today, I'm questioning if I need to close that door once and for all." Raven listens intently for your permission to continue. "What happened?" you ask. Raven lets out an almost inaudible sigh. "Okay, so I called Brenda today to ask her for five dollars. She lives two doors down from me, so I figured it shouldn't be a problem. I was hungry and my paycheck won't be deposited until midnight tomorrow. Instead of just saying no, she decided to give me a long lecture about how many times she's loaned me money. But, get this—I've always paid her back, so I don't see what the problem is! Anyhow, she started talking about not wanting to mix money with friendship, but here's my issue—if she needs my help, I'd give it to her! That's what friends are for, right? So, she said to me, 'Okay, I'll loan it to you this time, but just so you know, in the future, I will refrain from loaning you any more money.' What kind of friend is that?! And this isn't the first time that she's disrespected me like that! About two weeks ago, I was in the car with her when she pulled into the gas station. After pulling next to her favorite pump, she turned and looked at me with her big eyes, and then she put her hand out. I looked at her hand, and then at her. I asked her why she had her hand out, and she reminded me of twenty dollars that I borrowed from her like three months ago. I was hurt! I'd forgotten all about that measly twenty bucks! And doesn't the Bible say that love keeps no record of wrongs?! I'm just done with her! Before I cut all ties with her, I just needed to hear another person's point of view." What advice would you give her? First and foremost, I'd try to assess the nature of their relationship. How did they meet? What do they have in common today, as opposed to what they had in common when they met? What is the glue that holds their relationship together? Is it the fear of being alone? Is it truly love? Is it because they are two single women who don't know anything else to do with themselves besides entertain one another until a man comes along and separates them? Is it God that brought them together? The goal here is to determine if the relationship is directional or seasonal? Think of a directional relationship this way—imagine that you are divided into four quarters: north, south, east and west. Let's say that north represents career bonds; these are the bonds bought together by career-minded and/or ambitious people. And this isn't just limited to the career space. These types of bonds can and do form in any and every area where ambition lies (ex: churches, media, schools, etc.). The south represents relational bonds; these bonds include familial connections, romantic connections (people who bond over their desire to attract members of the opposite sex), trauma bonds, etc. The east represents financial bonds; these bonds have everything to do with classism and/or socioeconomic status, either actual or expected. The west represents religious bonds; these bonds are formed through religious beliefs. This would mean that Raven and Brenda may be east-side enemies, but in every other area of their lives, they may potentially get along. Simply put, it sounds like Raven is immature financially, and because she doesn't steward her finances well, she cannot be anyone's financial friend. Instead, in that particular area of her life, she is an exploiter. A better way to say this is—the east side of Raven's heart is a slum. Over time, Brenda came to realize that it was not a good idea to give or loan money to Raven, even though she considers Raven to be a great friend in every other area. But get this—by setting boundaries, Brenda is about to see if Raven is truly her friend. You see, people can be great friends in every other area if they are benefiting from the relationship in one area. The word "no" is the greatest test of a relationship, and as we can all see, Raven seems to be failing that test. Let's say that you explained to Raven that Brenda sounds like she is a terrific friend. She simply doesn't want to get into a financial entanglement (soul tie) with any of her friends. You say to Raven, "I don't think she's being malicious. I think that she's probably experienced offense a few times whenever you didn't return the money at the time she expected. For example, twenty dollars may not sound like a lot of money, but if she had to ask for it three months later, it means that you forgot to return it. And believe it or not, you've probably forgotten a few times, but even if you didn't, she just didn't like the way she felt whenever you borrowed money from her, so to protect the friendship, she decided to set a boundary in that area." Raven may humble herself after hearing your perspective. Then again, if she's prideful and entitled, chances are, she'll find a reason to get off the phone with you, and then she'll call someone who will agree with her. Either way, Brenda did a good thing when she placed that boundary around her finances, and while five dollars isn't a lot of money, no one likes to feel taken advantage of.

I had to learn this lesson myself. Whenever I asked God to send me a friend, He would always send someone who almost mirrored my love and loyalty in one area, but there were topics that we simply avoided. For example, I've had Christian friends who didn't have the same standards or convictions that I had in the area of romance. They didn't mind letting men come to their homes, nor did they mind kissing their boyfriends, but I made a decision to remove my foot from temptation, even reserving my first kiss with my future husband for our wedding day. For example, I have an amazing friend who I've never discussed the topic of sex and waiting for marriage with. I don't know if she's abstinent or what her convictions are in that area. I decided not to bring up that topic when I discovered that her convictions didn't align with mine. Again, I don't know if she's abstaining from sex, and if she is having sex, she may be a babe in Christ in that area. Have I spoke with her about my beliefs? Of course! I just never pried to see what hers were. Sometimes, the greatest ministry is through demonstration. And I can say this about her—she is an amazing friend in so many areas! All the same, I know that God placed her in my life, whether she's a directional friend or a seasonal one. Either way, she's still a fixture in my life, and I'm thankful for her. Another example is my mother. She passed away in 2018, but when she was alive, we simply could not talk about faith and religion. Sure, she was a Christian, but her beliefs didn't fully align with mine. Don't get me wrong; she was an amazing woman and mother, but she was definitely bound by Southern pride. What this means is, she was raised to believe that she was always right because she was the mother. In her days, children (whether young or old) could not question or challenge their parents, and she held tight to those beliefs. And she loved to bring up the topic of faith, but once I realized that we didn't get along in that area, I refused to have any theological discussions with her. You see, my mother was a babe in Christ and she was loyal to her denomination, so she would vehemently defend her denominational beliefs anytime we discussed religion. I can remember her asking me questions about the Bible, and I knew that she wasn't asking so that she could learn or so that we could have an amicable discussion about our beliefs. She simply had a set of beliefs that she wanted to introduce me to, and she didn't know how to go about starting this conversation, so she'd ask me about my beliefs. I still laugh today when I think about how those conversations went. She'd ask me a theological question, and I'd always say, "Nope, I'm not going there with you. You know we can't talk about religion, so let's just change the subject." She would then get offended and say something to the effect of, "I'm just asking a question. I'm truly curious. How do you expect me to learn if you refuse to answer any of my questions?" I knew better than that. I'd fallen into that trap one too many times, so I knew how that story would end. So, whenever this happened, I would hurriedly change the subject and then start closing the call if she tried to bring it back up. It didn't take her long to catch on, but I kept reminding her that we did not get along in that area. Anytime you find an area that you and another person do not and cannot align in because of pride, make sure you're the humble one and set boundaries in that area.

Let's talk about positional relationships. One thing I noticed, for example, on social media is that if I post a deep and revelatory message, there are certain people who will engage with that particular status. And because I tend to post a lot of Christian content, I've noticed that these people engage with my statuses often; some of them engage with eighty percent of my posts. Then again, there are some people who only engage with one to twenty percent of my posts, and I noticed that the posts they engage with are the funny ones or the ones where I'm just talking about life in general. For example, I might post up these two statuses:

- **Status One:** "God is love, so whenever someone says that they love you, they are saying that they have God's heart for you. If they don't have God's heart, they can't have God's heart for you."
- **Status Two:** "I went to the park today and ran into an old guy. Every time I turned around, he would look at me from behind. Offended, I shouted out, *Some people are too old to be so perverted*! I then got in my car and left. After that, I stopped by the grocery store to pick up a few items. When I got midways into the store, I saw another old guy looking at me from behind. I sighed, but right before I said anything, the man approached me and said, 'It looks like a bird got

ya!' I twisted my body to look at my pants, and
that's when I noticed a big white spot on my
black jogging pants. I must've sat in some bird
dung!"

The people who normally engage my deep posts will likely
engage the funny ones as well, but a lot of the people who
engage my general life posts do not engage my Christian
posts. And yes, many of them who do not engage are
Christians. Does this make them bad people? Nope. There
are many reasons that they may not engage my posts. For
one, I'm not that great at engaging with posts. Then again,
maybe they want a break from all of the religious talk or
they could be babes in Christ. All the same, they may not
agree with my perspective. It is possible that I may have
offended them with a few of my posts because I do speak
a lot about some of the customs and behaviors today that I
consider toxic. And, of course, I'd be silly to believe that
everyone who friend-requests me on social media actually
likes me. Nevertheless, I'm not bothered by a lack of
engagement because I've learned that there are heights
and depths to every topic, and people will engage you in a
conversation once you're in their neighborhood of thinking.
I'm a pattern's person. What I mean by this is, I'm wired to
see patterns. I don't do this intentionally. According to my
dad, I've always been this way. But being a person who
notices patterns, I tend to communicate with people in
accordance with where they are; that is unless I'm
mentoring or teaching them. For instance, if I noticed that
every time I spoke with you about the deep things of God,
you diverted your eyes and your body language told me

that you were trying to escape the conversation, I would learn your language. This is positional acuity or positional intelligence. I would change things up and have more of a surface-level conversation with you about God or, better yet, let you talk so that I could see where you are. You may be more mature and more knowledgeable than I am about the things of God; then again, the opposite may be true. Either way, if one of us has positional acuity, we could soon discover a way to connect with one another, even though our connection may not necessarily be an intimate one. Some of the most invaluable connections that you'll ever form are intellectual ones! This means that not everyone has to become your close friend or a friend at all! I believe that this is one of the reasons there are so many offended people walking the Earth today. The truth is—most people want to be "normal" and they want to be accepted. What this means is they want to fit in with whatever cultures, traditions and beliefs that the majority of people in their communities, schools, churches, families or peer groups have ascribed to. This is survivor's mode, and a lot of people live in it. The problem with this is— fitting in means that they are not graduating from one season to the next. This is because in order for them to fit in, they have to ensure that they never learn more than the people who serve as the principalities (instituters/sustainers of principles) of any given season. Another way to say this is—people exalt themselves. We know this. We saw this behavior in elementary, junior high and high school. We saw girl cliques led by young ladies whose only claim to fame were their wealthy fathers, but they themselves weren't going to do much in life. We just assumed that they too would be rich someday. So, they created girl-groups, and some of the people in these groups were smarter than they were, but they couldn't show it. Instead, some of these young ladies "dumbed themselves down" just to fit in. Consequently, they climaxed early in life. Some of them recovered after going to college or graduating, but some of them were bound by toxic loyalty. Understand this—you are never loyal to a person; you are always loyal to a mindset or, better yet, a season. Wait! What if you don't agree with that person? How can you then be loyal to a mindset? It's simple—you're loyal to the belief that by disconnecting from that person or demoting that person in your life that you are somehow a bad person when this is not true. The truth is—growth is marked by a notable movement of people in your life. As your mind changes, so will your circle. But if you refuse to leave old seasons behind to embrace new ones, you will become one of the masters of the season you're stuck in, and remember, another phrase for this is master manipulator or principality. Sure, we understand the concept of demonic principalities, but people can and often are the sustainers of principles as well. This is how cultures and traditions are established.

When utilizing positional acuity, you simply learn to be multidimensional in your conversations. And you can do this without being offended or offensive. So, if someone your age walks up to you and says something foolish or unintelligent, simply correct that person in love. Don't be condescending, and never correct someone in the presence of others unless that person is giving out information that can put others in danger. For example, if you're talking to a woman who claims that she was abducted by UFOs, and you're standing around with a group of people, don't engage in that conversation publicly, otherwise, you may humiliate her. On the other hand, if she says that UFOs told her that God doesn't exist, then correct her lovingly and right in front of the people. Why should you correct her publicly? To protect any babes in Christ or new believers from being led astray by her words. If everyone in the crowd is a mature believer, you may not have to correct her publicly; in this case, it's better to do so privately. If you have to correct her publicly, simply say, "Demons disguise themselves as everything from UFOs to angels of light. God does exist. That's why you're here and you're as beautiful as you are. And get this—God loves you. That's why He led you over this way." The goal here is to correct her in love and to avoid triggering the spirit of offense. Chances are, she will get offended because she's in need of deliverance. Then again, hearing you speak in love may cause her to open up her spirit to the truth. If she insists that she is right and is passionate about her beliefs, don't argue with her. Simply change the subject. Remember this—demons love to arouse your pride; this way, they can discredit anything you say without the intervention of God.

- **Proverbs 26:4:** Answer not a fool according to his folly, lest thou also be like unto him.
- **Proverbs 17:27-28:** He that hath knowledge spareth his words: and a man of understanding is of an excellent spirit. Even a fool, when he holdeth his peace, is counted wise: and he that

shutteth his lips is esteemed a man of understanding.

- **Proverbs 1:7:** The fear of the LORD is the beginning of knowledge: but fools despise wisdom and instruction.
- **James 4:6:** But he giveth more grace. Wherefore he saith, God resisteth the proud, but giveth grace unto the humble.

One sad fact I've noticed is—many of the people who are both broken and immature won't stick around long enough to allow themselves to be taught about the things of God. This is because they believe that everyone they value must be a part of their intimate circles. But because they don't understand rank and protocol (positional intelligence), they equalize every relationship, meaning they take people who outrank them and place them on their levels or lower. This may sound offensive to some people, but here's how that works—think of a name of a celebrity who is not considered to be all that intelligent (I won't name any). Now, imagine that the celebrity you chose is best friends with Albert Einstein. Envision that celebrity over-talking Einstein and insisting that he or she is right about everything, and Dr. Einstein absolutely has to follow that celebrity's lead. Doesn't that look too much like a four-year old bossing around a college student? Read this and record it in your heart—anytime you come in contact with someone who does not rank as high as you intellectually or spiritually, that person will try to control you if he or she is immature and broken. Think about it. Every person who has ever tried to dominate or bully you wasn't as smart as you were. Instead, they tried to control the conversation by only speaking on the topics they wanted to speak on; they got angry when you presented facts to them, especially if you could prove those facts, and they either spoke over you, twisted your words or yelled at you whenever you challenged something they'd said. Some of them may have even attempted to fight you. This typically happens when you get stuck in or are about to graduate from a realm or a region of thought and you come across some of the principalities of that season. They will insist on being your friend, all the while, attempting to bully and dominate you. They not only lack positional acuity, they are not interested in growing their knowledge base; they simply want to look better and sound smarter than everyone around them. And because they can't do this, they tend to silence everyone by yelling or putting people on punishment. Again, unbeknownst to them, these people are practicing relational witchcraft, and you have to be mindful that you don't allow yourself to get entangled with them. And definitely don't allow them to get into your intimate circle, because it's not easy to get them out of it. Beware of people who insist on being the smartest people in their circles, especially when they clearly aren't!

Seasonal and Conditional Acuity

Let's talk about seasonal acuity. What's sad is that many of us make permanent friends out of seasonal connections. Consider the marriage between Samson and his first wife. Let's look at a few snippets of their story.

- **Judges 14:1-4:** And Samson went down to Timnath, and saw a woman in Timnath of the daughters of the Philistines. And he came up, and told his father and his mother, and said, I have seen a woman in Timnath of the daughters of the Philistines: now therefore get her for me to wife. Then his father and his mother said unto him, Is there never a woman among the daughters of thy brethren, or among all my people, that thou goest to take a wife of the uncircumcised Philistines? And Samson said unto his father, Get her for me; for she pleaseth me well. But his father and his mother knew not that it was of the LORD, that he sought an occasion against the Philistines: for at that time the Philistines had dominion over Israel.

- **Judges 14:8-20:** And after a time he returned to take her, and he turned aside to see the carcass of the lion: and, behold, there was a swarm of bees and honey in the carcass of the lion. And he took thereof in his hands, and went on eating, and came to his father and mother, and he gave them, and they did eat: but he told not them that he had taken the honey out of the carcass of the lion. So his father went down unto the woman: and Samson made there a feast; for so used the young men to do. And it came to pass, when they saw him, that they brought thirty companions to be with him. And Samson said unto them, I will now put forth a riddle unto you: if ye can certainly declare it me within the seven days of the feast, and find it out, then I will give you thirty sheets and thirty change of garments: But if ye cannot declare it me, then shall ye give me thirty sheets and thirty change of garments. And they said unto him, Put forth thy riddle, that we may hear it. And he said unto them, Out of the eater came forth meat, and out of the strong came forth sweetness. And they could not in three days expound the riddle. And it came to pass on the seventh day, that they said unto Samson's wife, Entice thy husband, that he may declare unto us the riddle, lest we burn thee and thy father's house with fire: have ye called us to take that we have? Is it not so? And Samson's wife wept before him, and said, Thou dost but hate me, and lovest me not: thou hast put forth a riddle unto the children of my people, and hast not told it me. And he said unto her, Behold, I have not told it my father nor my mother, and shall I tell it thee? And she wept before him the seven days, while their feast lasted: and it came to pass on the seventh day, that he told her, because she lay sore upon him: and she told the riddle to the children of her people. And the men of the city said unto him on the seventh day before the sun went down, What is sweeter than honey?

and what is stronger than a lion? And he said unto them, If ye had not plowed with my heifer, ye had not found out my riddle. And the Spirit of the LORD came upon him, and he went down to Ashkelon, and slew thirty men of them, and took their spoil, and gave change of garments unto them which expounded the riddle. And his anger was kindled, and he went up to his father's house. But Samson's wife was given to his companion, whom he had used as his friend.

- **Judges 15:1:** But it came to pass within a while after, in the time of wheat harvest, that Samson visited his wife with a kid; and he said, I will go in to my wife into the chamber. But her father would not suffer him to go in. And her father said, I verily thought that thou hadst utterly hated her; therefore I gave her to thy companion: is not her younger sister fairer than she? take her, I pray thee, instead of her.

This act initiated a war between Samson and the Philistines. Of course, this story is about Samson and his first wife; this is the woman he married before meeting Delilah. According to the scriptures, God instituted this relationship between Samson and this particular woman so that He could have an occasion or opportunity to bring down the Philistines. The Lord knew what would happen; her loyalty was to her people. This means that her position in Samson's life was seasonal. But the mistake that Samson made was this—he essentially divorced that woman, but he didn't divorce the demon that was in that woman. This is why he was so attracted to Delilah.

Many of the relationships that we find ourselves in were only designed to be seasonal, but there is a spiritual connection between us and everyone we connect ourselves to. This is because we are spirits living in bodies. Our conversations may be surface-level, but whenever spirits commune, a world of words is created that connects them with one another. This is especially true for intimate connections. Believe it or not, we have all instituted many verbal contracts with people without even realizing what we were doing. We've promised people:

1. Spots in our future weddings.
2. That we'll never leave them.
3. That they'll always have a place in our hearts.
4. To make them rich if we ever got rich.

And then, those relationships ended. Howbeit, unbeknownst to us, words are spirit, meaning they don't just dissipate or evaporate into thin air. We have to address whatever it is or was that we've said. We do this by repenting, apologizing and making a different declaration, not just with our mouths, but with our choices.

Nowadays, it's more common to see people holding onto seasonal relationships out of fear, toxic loyalty and a sense of obligation than it is to see people chasing the full heart of God. And get this—I'm not saying that we should be running around discarding our friends every time our I.Q.

grows by a point or two. It simply means that we shouldn't be afraid to grow wiser, smarter or more independent. All the same, when we recognize the difference between a seasonal connection and a permanent one, we will spend less time healing and more time being productive. How do you know if a relationship is seasonal?

1. **When the focus of the relationship is centered around a seasonal issue.** For example, let's say that there is a tree that the city wants to cut down. You may be protesting the cutting down of that tree, and you meet someone who is also fighting for the tree. Once the bill is passed and the fate of the tree is established, you may never see or talk with that person again.

2. **When the relationship is centered around a common threat or enemy.** This one is pretty self-explanatory, but in short, let's say that you're about to take your ex to court for child support, and one of the women who has a child with him decides to become one of your allies. Your relationship with her may be seasonal, even though your children are siblings. After the court session is over, she may never speak with you again or she may become an enemy of yours.

3. **When the relationship is centered around a need.** For example, you may be a broke college student trying to make ends meet, and you may meet another broke college student who is also struggling to get by. The two of you may discover that you're better off rooming together and mixing your funds together. Once the two of you graduate,

you may never speak again. Unfortunately, a lot of romantic relationships are built on this particular foundation, which is why divorce rates are so high.

4. **When the relationship is centered around a void.** You may be lonely, and you may come across someone who doesn't feel validated unless he or she is in a relationship. Remember, voids are black holes in the soul that create a force called attraction. This attraction could draw you to that particular person. And I always warn people of this—once God heals that person's void, he or she won't be attracted to their lovers anymore.

5. **When the relationship is centered around an erroneous belief.** Consider some of the religious beliefs that are prevalent today. There are many false and oppressive religions on this planet, and the people who ascribe to them actually meet people in those religions and marry them.

Of course, any of these relationships can be permanent, but the only way to know if a relationship is God-approved is to:

1. Keep growing. Never climax in a region of thought.
2. Keep God first. Submit to His Word and resist the temptation of the enemy (see James 4:7).
3. Say "no" sometimes. Don't feel obligated to give people what they want when they want it just because they want it. People who love you will respect your wishes; people who are benefiting from you will walk away when those benefits dry up.

4. Set boundaries and enforce them. Never submit yourself to toxic loyalty.

5. Do what God told you to do. I've noticed that people who were called to build (write books, launch businesses, etc.) often surround themselves with time-wasters. These are people who have no vision and no earthly ambition outside of connecting to and riding the skirt-tails of successful people. Consequently, those called and chosen by God often fall behind or even deny their assignments in an attempt to maintain those relationships.

Also note that some of the greatest relationships are the ones where you are the teacher in one area and the student in another. This means that you may find yourself connecting with people who, for example, are smarter than you are in the world of entrepreneurship, but they may not be as wise as you are in the world of faith. Relationships like these are invaluable and they require a great deal of relational acuity, maturity and humility. This is because the both of you have to know when to lead and when to follow. All too often, in relationships like these, one of the parties involved becomes too prideful and refuses to relinquish the lead when the time calls for it. All the same, you may find yourself intimately connected in one area and intellectually connected in another, but again, relationships like these require a great deal of spiritual acuity and humility. All the same, some of the most toxic relationships are the ones where you have to be the teacher in every area and the student doesn't recognize or acknowledge that he or she is a student. That's pride—

prideful and entitled people are some of the most dangerous souls on the planet because they don't have ears to hear, therefore, they will not listen to the voice of reason. Prideful people are like children who insist on having their way in a conversation and exalting their opinions over the voices of those who are more experienced and wiser than they are. Like children, they throw tantrums and speak over anyone who tries to impart wisdom into them. Remember, whenever you come across a subject that is too sensitive for you to speak about with another person, change the subject. In that area, the two of you may never be friends. But beware! If a person is way too passionate about a matter, changing the subject won't change their views of you. I learned the following the hard way:

1. Some people are committed to misunderstanding you.

2. Stay away from people who wrestle with jealousy and competition, after all, you can't talk a demon out of being a demon.

3. Stay away from people who are easily offended by you. Wherever you find the spirit of offense, you will also find the spirits of control and witchcraft. You may even find the Jezebel spirit.

4. While you may have a lot in common in one or more areas, some people's hatred for you in other areas is far too great to give them access to you.

5. Sometimes, the greatest gift you can give a person is your absence or, at minimum, distance. Get this— every Christian is a beacon of light. Some of our lights shine brighter than others, and demons hate

light! I've literally watched people be tormented by demons whenever they were too close to me. For example, they'll start having a bunch of evil thoughts about me; they'll start thinking that everything I post on social media or preach is about them or they'll misinterpret everything I do. All too often, they may even feel the need to compete. When I see this behavior, I know to put space, time and distance between me and the person. Sadly enough, it often turns into one of those "darned if you do, darned if you don't" type situations. What I mean by this is—if and whenever I allowed them to walk close to me, they were tormented and frustrated, but when I put them in my intellectual circle, they were offended and felt rejected. I soon learned that demonized people will be mad at you no matter where you place them. They'll be offended if they can't get close enough to sabotage and/or destroy you, or they'll be offended if they are close enough to see God blessing you. The best gift to give them is space.

6. Anytime you allow a person to usurp authority over you just because they feel entitled to it, you have effectively become an Ahab (one of Jezebel's puppets).

7. Toxic relationships are demonic institutions that house those who don't yet know their worth.

8. You can love people who hate you, but it won't change the fact that they hate you. Hateful people hate God, even when they claim to love Him. 1 John 4:20 says it this way, "If a man say, I love God, and

hateth his brother, he is a liar: for he that loveth
not his brother whom he hath seen, how can he love
God whom he hath not seen?"

Now, let's talk about conditional affiliates or relationships.
Let's face it. Some relationships are conditional. This
means that they serve a single purpose or a series of
purposes, but once those objectives or conditions have
been met, the relationships fizzle. We have to get
delivered from thinking that every conditional relationship
is a bad one or that we were taken advantage of. This line
of reasoning sets the stage for us to form permanent
connections from relationships that were only designed to
serve a single purpose. A good example of a conditional
relationship is the one that David had with the king's
butler. Let's look at a couple of scriptures.

- **Genesis 40:9-15:** And the chief butler told his
  dream to Joseph, and said to him, In my dream,
  behold, a vine was before me; And in the vine were
  three branches: and it was as though it budded, and
  her blossoms shot forth; and the clusters thereof
  brought forth ripe grapes: And Pharaoh's cup was in
  my hand: and I took the grapes, and pressed them
  into Pharaoh's cup, and I gave the cup into
  Pharaoh's hand. And Joseph said unto him, This is
  the interpretation of it: The three branches are
  three days: Yet within three days shall Pharaoh lift
  up thine head, and restore thee unto thy place: and
  thou shalt deliver Pharaoh's cup into his hand, after
  the former manner when thou wast his butler. But
  think on me when it shall be well with thee, and

shew kindness, I pray thee, unto me, and make mention of me unto Pharaoh, and bring me out of this house: For indeed I was stolen away out of the land of the Hebrews: and here also have I done nothing that they should put me into the dungeon.

- **Genesis 41:9-13:** Then spake the chief butler unto Pharaoh, saying, I do remember my faults this day: Pharaoh was wroth with his servants, and put me in ward in the captain of the guard's house, both me and the chief baker: And we dreamed a dream in one night, I and he; we dreamed each man according to the interpretation of his dream. And there was there with us a young man, an Hebrew, servant to the captain of the guard; and we told him, and he interpreted to us our dreams; to each man according to his dream he did interpret. And it came to pass, as he interpreted to us, so it was; me he restored unto mine office, and him he hanged.

Of course, we know the rest of that story. Pharaoh sent for Joseph, and by the grace of God, Joseph was able to interpret Pharaoh's dreams. This pleased the king so much that he made Joseph second in charge. In other words, Joseph became the prime minister of Egypt. This means that Joseph's relationship with the butler turned cup-bearer was conditional. Once those conditions were met, the purpose of their relationship had been fulfilled. Of course, the men likely ran into one another after Joseph was promoted, but the Bible does not mention a long-standing relationship with the men. As a matter of fact, relationships between men of high rank with men who served under them (fraternization) has always been both frowned upon and discouraged to preserve the integrity of the kingdom or organization that the men served. The goal was to discourage familiarity and to protect highly sensitive information that men of higher rank had been entrusted with. You see, people often honor, respect and submit to those who outrank them when they don't have a personal connection to them. This is why the military and most companies have what is referred to as the standards of conduct. Men and women of rank can be severely punished for fraternizing with the people under their command because most establishments want to protect themselves from:

1. **Allegations of Favoritism**. Most companies and organizations want to discourage favoritism as it may compromise the integrity and rip the moral fabric of their establishments.

2. **Dishonor**. Most people cannot and will not honor those who they are familiar with. This is because a lot of people don't know how to have hierarchical relationships when they are the underlings in those relationships. In other words, they will attempt to equalize or balance out any relationship that they find themselves a part of. This removes the head (leader) and stops both people from elevating. All the same, most people who attempt to equalize relationships don't want equality; they are oftentimes controlling. Their objective is to control the person or people that they should be gleaning from.

3. **Morale**. The people who do not have a close relationship with the leaders who are guilty of fraternization will often feel that the person or people who are fraternizing with the leaders are unfairly favored and thereby granted access to certain freedoms and benefits that they themselves cannot access. This causes the morale in the workplace or organization to diminish; it also promotes division and dishonor.

Why are we talking about fraternization? Because a lot of relationships that you will find yourself in will involve people who outrank you and vice versa. In order for you to extract the full benefits of those relationships, you have to understand rank and how to properly respond to it. All the same, if you come across someone who God wants you to pour into, but that person insists on equalizing the relationship, you have to take a step back and help the individual to understand the concept of rank, regardless of whether the relationship is directional, positional, seasonal or conditional. If you allow the person to dictate and lead the relationship when he or she is not spiritually mature enough to do so, that person will lead you into bondage. Matthew 15:12-14 reads, "Then came his disciples, and said unto him, Knowest thou that the Pharisees were offended, after they heard this saying? But he answered and said, Every plant, which my heavenly Father hath not planted, shall be rooted up. Let them alone: they be blind leaders of the blind. And if the blind lead the blind, both shall fall into the ditch." The ditch is a low place; it is a valley of sorts and a place of darkness. In the aforementioned scripture, we find the disciples warning Jesus about the Pharisees. You see, the issue with the Pharisees was that they wanted to lead Jesus; they didn't want to be led by Him. They wanted to lead Him into religion, whereas He was trying to lead them out of the Old Testament law and into an intimate relationship with God. The problem was all about control. People tend to hate those who they cannot control. I have had my fair share of people who've come to me wanting mentorship, only for them to throw tantrums and leave my mentorship program when they couldn't have their way. I've learned one of the most sinister traps that people set is this—they will try to find a need, a void or a place in your life that they can serve in. They will then try to create a demand for themselves by filling those voids, fulfilling those needs or going above and beyond the call of duty to assist. Once they believe that they've successfully created a demand for themselves or a soul tie with you, they'll start making their own demands and threatening you with their absence. This bait and hook method is relatively common nowadays, and it is a form of relational witchcraft. You see, people like this are so afraid of rejection that they feel the need to control every relationship that they are a part of, especially the ones they consider to be invaluable. So, they may volunteer to make your enemies their enemies, they may assist you in rearranging your home or they may help you out financially, but everything they do for you has motives attached to it. In other words, it's bait. You see, they understand that most people are bound by toxic reciprocity. The way that toxic reciprocity works is:

1. There are people who overprice every moment and everything that you do for them. For example, if you straighten up their hair when it's messy, buy them a meal when they're hungry, pick them up when they don't have a vehicle or encourage them when they're down, they will feel like they owe you their lives.
2. They will keep trying to pay you back by giving you their time and resources.
3. They require the bare minimum as it relates to friendship. They'll give you almost everything that's valuable to them, and they will value anything that you give to them, no matter how minuscule it is.

These people are prophetic producers in their infant stages. In short, they have the gift of charity; this is the gift of love that compels people to give. Givers typically don't know how to stop giving; that is until they become producers. Howbeit, most of them never reach the producers' stage because they are traumatized by consumers before they can even understand their giftings and/or their assignments.

Another example of conditional affiliation is Esther's marriage to King Ahasuerus (also believed to be King Xerxes I). Ordinarily, marriage between Jews and Gentiles was prohibited; it was even against the Old Testament law. Nevertheless, God arranged the events that would lead to Esther's ordination. The objective here was to save the Jews because God knew that a wicked man by the name of Haman was somewhere being broken and twisted by the enemy so that he would grow up to become the murderous, Jew-hating Jezebel that he was. Had it not been for Esther, the Jews in Persia would have been annihilated. And while their marriage may have lasted a long time, it was a conditional marriage, meaning that it was only brought together to serve a single purpose. Once that purpose was fulfilled, their relationship was fulfilled. There's no telling what came of that relationship. If King Ahasuerus is truly King Xerxes I, as many scholars believe him to be (which he more than likely was), his marriage to Esther took place in 478 BC and he was killed in 465 BC. This means that if this information is true, their marriage lasted for 13 years before the king was effectively dethroned by death.

Conditional relationships are relationships that ordinarily would not form, but are established because of a working set of conditions or problems that have to be solved. Many of these also fall under the category of seasonal relationships, while others are lifelong. All the same, some of these relationships are God-established, while others are either demonic or carnal. Consider the relationship between Hosea and Gomer. Look at the following scriptures.

- **Hosea 1:2-3:** The beginning of the word of the LORD by Hosea. And the LORD said to Hosea, Go, take unto thee a wife of whoredoms and children of whoredoms: for the land hath committed great whoredom, departing from the LORD. So he went and took Gomer the daughter of Diblaim; which conceived, and bare him a son.

- **Hosea 3:** Then said the LORD unto me, Go yet, love a woman beloved of her friend, yet an adulteress, according to the love of the LORD toward the children of Israel, who look to other gods, and love flagons of wine. So I bought her to me for fifteen pieces of silver, and for an homer of barley, and an half homer of barley: And I said unto her, Thou shalt abide for me many days; thou shalt not play the harlot, and thou shalt not be for another man: so will I also be for thee. For the children of Israel shall abide many days without a king, and without a prince, and without a sacrifice, and without an image, and without an ephod, and without teraphim: Afterward shall the children of Israel return, and seek the LORD their God, and David their king; and shall fear the LORD and his goodness in the latter days.

Again, the goal of a conditional relationship is to serve a specific purpose. An example of a carnal one is the relationship between David and Bathsheba. The sole and initial purpose of that relationship was to satisfy David's lustful appetite. You see, he'd seen Bathsheba bathing on the roof of her house, and after inquiring about her, he discovered that she was a married woman. This didn't phase him, however, because his lust for her overrode his desire to please God in that moment. He sent some of his guards to bring her to him, and from there, he slept with her. Bathsheba became pregnant, and when David heard the news, he panicked. For one, his reputation would have taken a near fatal blow, especially with him being the king of Israel. And two, Old Testament law dictated that both he and Bathsheba be stoned to death for their crime (see Deuteronomy 22:22, Leviticus 20:10). In his attempt to control the outcome and stagnate the system of sowing and reaping, David sent for Uriah, Bathsheba's husband, hoping that he would go home and sleep with his wife. Instead, Uriah was a giver; his love and loyalty to the king ran so deep that he denied himself the pleasure of sleeping with his wife. Because of this, David behaved like his former master, Saul, towards Uriah. He had the man killed, and then to hide his sin from the eyes of Israel, he hurried up and married Bathsheba. Nevertheless, God saw what he'd done, and David paid a hefty price for his sin against God and his sin against Uriah.

It's frustrating for most of us when we realize that a relationship that we are a part of is a conditional one, but again, not all conditional relationships are carnal or demonic. Some of them are God-instituted. In short, they may grow into intimate relationships and then slowly retrogress into intellectual relationships; that's when you'll see the person in passing from time to time. Don't make this person your enemy, even if the individual spitefully used you. Instead, be proactive instead of reactive whenever you begin to form a bond with another person. You do this by praying this prayer:

> "Lord, place (individual's name) in my life where you want him or her to be, and not where I want (individual's name) to be, and place (individual's name) in my life where you want him/her to be. Don't let me give (individual's name) any roles,

responsibilities, expectations or titles that he/she cannot function in, and don't allow me to accept any roles, responsibilities, expectations or titles that I cannot function in. Give us relational intelligence as it relates to one another, and let Your will be done in our relationship, and not our own. If (individual's name) has been sent by the enemy or if our relationship is carnal, turn the tables and let your name be glorified in this relationship if it is Your will. If this is not Your will, drive (person's name) out of my life, and close the door between us. Also, reveal to me the open doors in my life that need to be shut and show me how to shut them. I surrender my will to Your will, in Jesus' name."

After you've said this prayer, don't rush the relationship and don't allow the person to rush into your intimate space. Take your time so that you can hear back from God. All the same, if the relationship goes against the Word of God, you don't have to pray about it because the answer was already given to you in His Word. Set boundaries, enforce them, be patient and be led by the Lord.

Learning and acknowledging the differences between directional, positional, seasonal and conditional relationships can save you a lot of time and money, and this can save you from a lot of heartache. It can even save your life! The most frustrating part of this is—when you master the difference, chances are, the people around you will not understand why you are not engaging them in some areas or why you had to distance yourself from them in other areas, but you cannot and should never subject yourself to someone else's belief system or season when it is contrary to or contradicts the Word of God. Those same people will give you a hard time when they don't understand why they can't serve in the roles or positions they want to serve in, but years later, when they enter into the season you're in, they'll say, "Oh, I understand now why you said what you said or did what you did." And if you'd held yourself back for them, you will have relinquished God's trust in favor of them catching up. God can only trust you when you follow and obey Him with so much vigor that you are willing to forsake any and every relationship and/or connection to uplift His name!

Note: some parent/children relationships are conditional. The parents' only job was to bring those people into the world, but once they were done, they didn't know how to raise the children, how to care for them or how to properly steward their gifts/anointings. Consequently, many of these children grow up traumatized, but what many of them don't realize is this—they were raised in the systems that they were designed to destroy. In other words, they have an advantage over others who are trying to dismantle those systems because they themselves understand the inner-workings of those systems.

STANDARDS OF COMMUNICATION

I have a mentorship program that consists of well over one hundred women, and while this program is filled with beautiful, anointed and amazing women, I've come across my fair share of broken women. This is okay, after all, this is what I'm there for. However, broken people break people —or, at least, they try to. I've had a few incidents where I've received condescending and offensive emails from some of the former students. They'd tell me that they no longer want to be a part of my program, throw out a few insults and go out of their way to make me feel what they're feeling in that moment. In truth, I don't read offensive emails. Once I see the first insult, I click the reply button and say, for example, "Yes ma'am. God bless you" or "Be blessed!" There have been instances where I'd responded with a simple "okay," and then there were times when I didn't respond at all. This is because they all know my standard of communication. I don't engage in toxic, condescending or offensive conversations. I believe that it's okay to be offended, but before you reach out to the person you are offended with, you should follow through a process that I call "sorting."

What is sorting? Think about laundry. When you were younger, chances are, your parent or guardian would wash a load of clothes, and once those clothes were dry, he or she would fold and separate them. They'd separate everyone's clothes and put them in a stack before calling you all into their bedroom or living room to pick up your stack of clothes. This is called sorting. We sort through laundry to determine what belongs to us and what belongs to others.

When someone offends you, the first thing you must do is sort. You see, if you rush over to a person and start telling that individual that you're offended and why you are offended, you will likely deal with the humiliation of having that person point out a detail you've overlooked. For example, imagine that you called a friend of yours and said, "I saw what you posted on social media! I know you were talking about me! Why would you talk about dandruff when I just told you that I've been dealing with it? I'm done with you!" After you were done speaking, you hung up the phone and declared in your mind that the friendship was over. Ten minutes later, you receive a long text from your now former friend. She said, "In my post, I simply suggested a dandruff shampoo that I use to control my dandruff. I didn't mention you, nor did I think about you. I shared that post because your baby sister reached out to me to find out what shampoo I've been using. Remember, she does my hair! And she noticed that I haven't been having problems with dandruff for about a month now. I offered to text the image to her phone, but she said that she'd broken her screen and couldn't see it. I offered to inbox her the picture, but she said that another friend of hers wanted to know what it is also, and that friend follows my Facebook page. So, she asked me to share it on my page. But thank you for showing me how you feel about me. It was nice knowing you and I wish you nothing but the best."

The first level of sorting is to determine whether or not you should be offended. This requires you to examine the offense carefully and consider the character of the person you're offended with. Then, you have to ask yourself these three questions:

1. Is my offense justifiable or am I overreacting?
2. Am I going through something that is potentially causing me to be super-sensitive?
3. Am I already offended by this person and am I looking for a way to express my frustration?

The second part of sorting is examination. This is when you have to examine yourself for jealousy, unforgiveness and fear. Have you engaged in any gossip about the person? Are your expectations realistic or unrealistic? Examine them and be honest with yourself. Also, look at your history with this person. Is this a repeated offense, and if so, have you directly communicated with the person about it? For example, most of the students who became offended with me had unrealistic expectations when they'd signed up for my mentorship program. They'd envisioned me mentoring them and them only, and many of them didn't know the differences between mentorship, coaching and counseling. They wanted individualized attention, and some of them did not fare well around other women. And obviously, I can't fully blame all of them. I had to realize over time that I needed to learn to better communicate what people would be getting from my program and what they would not be getting. Additionally, I had to become better at listening to their needs and looking for ways to help them with those needs.

The next part of the process is called consideration. What is the person going through right now? Is it possible that you've offended the individual in question? You have to consider all the variables surrounding the offense and everything else that may be taking place in the other person's life.

The third and most important part of the process is accountability. What role did you play in the offense? Try empathizing with the other individual in this. Take responsibility for what you did wrong; it helps to lower the guard of the person you're offended with should you choose to address the offense with that person. Talk to the individual and take responsibility for your roles in the offense before you hand them their stack of offenses. And don't just hand them a bunch of problems, give them solutions! For example, after taking responsibility for what I've done wrong or how I may have contributed to the offense, I may say, "I have a solution. Instead of you raising your voice at me on the work floor, try setting up an impromptu meeting with me after you've calmed down." This is far better than saying, "I'm not going to warn you again! Stop raising your voice at me! I'm not your kid!" What you may not realize, for example, is that the person in question may have lost his one and only child a few years prior.

Use this method in intimate relationships. Let's say that you're married and your spouse offends you by not coming home at what you deem to be a respectable hour. Don't threaten your spouse; don't show hostility. Your first assignment is to listen. After this, offer up a solution. For example, try saying something to the effect of, "I understand that your friends weren't ready to come home because they are single, but remember, you have a wife at home. Staying out late only serves to birth distrust. So, let's try this. Consider hanging out with your married friends more and you should initiate hanging out with your single friends less; this way, you can schedule something earlier. What do you think, or do you have any other suggestions?" In this, the spouse doesn't feel controlled, manipulated or castrated. All the same, your spouse is more likely to follow a set of rules that he or she has set and/or agreed to.

Sorting helps you to better communicate with the people in your life and in your circle. It also helps to reveal just how mature the people around you are. And it goes without saying that you don't have to sort out every offense. Some offenses are blatant and may need to be immediately addressed. In cases like that, just be prayerful, logical and ethical.

I set boundaries around myself a long time ago, and it pretty much served as an enema in my life. I soon discovered that many of the people I tolerated were also tolerating me. I also discovered a Kingdom principle. That is—when people are in their proper places in your life, the blessings will flow to you and through you without incident. One of the boundaries I set was a standard of communication, and of course, I started with my family. My standard of communication pretty much says:

- No one can raise their voice at me. We must remain calm and respectable.
- No one is allowed to call me out of my name.
- No condescending words or tones about me or anyone I am affiliated with (this includes friends, love interests, pastors, etc.).
- Gaslighting is illegal.
- Witchcraft and control are illegal; this includes manipulation.
- No gossip or slander.

These are just a few examples. So, if a relative of mine, for example, raises his or her voice at me, my first response would be, "Please don't raise your voice at me, otherwise, I'll hang up. This is my first and only warning. I don't mind discussing the matter if we can do so respectfully." If the relative continues to raise his or her voice, I would simply hang up the phone, and I wouldn't take any more of that relative's calls that day. I wouldn't listen to voice messages or read text messages from that relative either since he or she is hellbent on hurting and offending me. I would also reconsider that relative's position in my life. Is he or she too close? Has he or she been warned before about this behavior?

Believe it or not, setting a standard of communication is not easy at first because most of the time, we are having to communicate these boundaries and standards to people who are used to disrespecting us. And it is hard for them to:

1. Break that habit.

2. Take us seriously.
3. Have a healthy conversation that does not involve emotional witchcraft and control.

Nevertheless, it may be difficult for them, but it's not impossible. Every person who loves you will respect your boundaries. All the same, you can't be a hypocrite. You must also keep a calm tone, be respectable and not use any of the mechanisms of control. If you require people to respect you when you don't respect them, you are asking them to come under your control, and of course, this is witchcraft. God gave us all the freedom of will, and even He does not override it, even though He's perfect in all His ways! So, how silly is it for an imperfect, mentally unstable person to demand the ability to control others?! Nevertheless, we see this everyday; it is now commonplace all over the world. Demon-possessed and oppressed people are oftentimes hellbent on controlling other people, whether that's through the means of dominant control or passive control. Either way, it's ungodly behavior.

Here's where things may get a little crazy! For some people, especially close relatives, you may have to publish your boundaries; that is if they violate them after you've communicated them. What does this look like? I would probably send a text message that reads:

> "Hi, amazing one! I hope this text finds you well and I hope your day is as amazing as you are! And please note that the goal of this message is NOT to offend. Instead, my goal is to preserve and maybe even

grow my relationship with you. With that being said, I have decided to make some changes to my life so that I can be healthier mentally, emotionally and spiritually. We all have to hit the reset button every now and again; right? Anyhow, I have a new standard of communication that I want to make you aware of since we've had trouble navigating some of our conversations in the past. And let me start off with apologizing for any time I may have said something disrespectful or used the wrong tone with you. I sincerely love and honor you, and I want you to feel that in our relationship. With that being said, for all future communications, let's refrain from the following:

1. Profanity.
2. Condescending remarks.
3. Gossip/Slander.
4. Elevated tones.
5. Name-calling.
6. Passive aggressiveness.
7. Any other behavior that may be offensive.

In short, let's be intentional because that's what healthy relationships are made of! And just so you are aware, I won't accept or tolerate any of these behaviors starting now, and I don't expect you to tolerate them from me. Let's exemplify love in everything that we do! I love you and I pray that you were able to read this message in the spirit in which I sent it because I truly do value our relationship!"

Unfortunately, when you're dealing with toxic, narcissistic or broken people who are determined to control you, such a message will not be received well because, once again, bound people hate boundaries. They will, instead, accuse you of trying to control them. This is oftentimes because they don't have the proper labels for this since they have rarely, if ever, come across boundaries in their personal or platonic relationships. So, this boundary is not only foreign to them, it will oftentimes be so offensive that they'll likely share the text message with other family members or friends, especially the ones who are closest to you and the ones who abhor you. They will avoid, at all costs, anyone who demonstrates sound reasoning. Nevertheless, you cannot carry the burden of their offense. And if they remove themselves from your life, just know that James 4:7 just took effect. It reads, "Submit yourselves therefore to God. Resist the devil, and he will flee from you." In other words, folks who have the devil in them will leave your life, and this is okay! Boundaries cause people to get into the roles and positions that they're mature enough to handle, and they remove them from the roles and responsibilities that they've elected themselves for.

Always have a standard of communication with everyone you exchange numbers with, and communicate those boundaries whenever the moment calls for it.

THE GIFT OF CHARITY

Most of us are familiar with the entirety of 1 Corinthians 13 since it is the most read book at weddings. It reads, "Though I speak with the tongues of men and of angels, and have not charity, I am become as sounding brass, or a tinkling cymbal. And though I have the gift of prophecy, and understand all mysteries, and all knowledge; and though I have all faith, so that I could remove mountains, and have not charity, I am nothing. And though I bestow all my goods to feed the poor, and though I give my body to be burned, and have not charity, it profiteth me nothing. Charity suffereth long, and is kind; charity envieth not; charity vaunteth not itself, is not puffed up, Doth not behave itself unseemly, seeketh not her own, is not easily provoked, thinketh no evil; rejoiceth not in iniquity, but rejoiceth in the truth; beareth all things, believeth all things, hopeth all things, endureth all things. Charity never faileth: but whether there be prophecies, they shall fail; whether there be tongues, they shall cease; whether there be knowledge, it shall vanish away. For we know in part, and we prophesy in part. But when that which is perfect is come, then that which is in part shall be done away. When I was a child, I spake as a child, I understood as a child, I thought as a child: but when I became a man, I put away childish things. For now we see through a glass, darkly; but then face to face: now I know in part; but then shall I know even as also I am known. And now abideth faith, hope, charity, these three; but the greatest of these is charity." Encyclopedia Britannica reports the following about "charity":

> "Charity: in Christian thought, the highest form of
> love, signifying the reciprocal love between God and
> man that is made manifest in unselfish love of one's
> fellow men. St. Paul's classical description of charity
> is found in the New Testament (I Cor. 13). In
> Christian theology and ethics, charity (a translation
> of the Greek word agapē, also meaning "love") is
> most eloquently shown in the life, teachings, and
> death of Jesus Christ. St. Augustine summarized
> much of Christian thought about charity when he
> wrote: "Charity is a virtue which, when our
> affections are perfectly ordered, unites us to God,
> for by it we love him." Using this definition and
> others from the Christian tradition, the medieval
> theologians, especially St. Thomas Aquinas, placed
> charity in the context of the other Christian virtues
> and specified its role as "the foundation or root" of
> them all (Source: Encyclopedia
> Britannica/Charity/Christian Concept).

Every relationship, be it intimate or intellectual, is
established on a set of principles or beliefs. For example, I
often come in contact with people who've had the dishonor
and displeasure of hosting people in their lives who were
takers, and by takers, I mean that they were not reciprocal
in any shape, form or fashion. In other words, they were
consumers. The people I'd run into, on the other hand,
were producers or solutionists. What I've come to realize is
that most producers are truly rare and unique. Every time I
come across someone who fits this particular category and

we speak over the phone, we end up talking for hours. Here are a few of the similarities I've discovered that many, if not most, producers have:

1. They're givers in a world filled with takers, so they've dealt with their fair share of trauma.

2. Producers unwittingly give or finance their way out of relationships. Don't get me wrong; they LOVE helping people. Howbeit, most producers soon discover that a large majority of people don't know how to control themselves whenever they come in contact with givers, so they'll not only keep taking (if allowed), but they'll start feeling entitled to what belongs to the producer. This is why producers are oftentimes discarded when they start setting boundaries around their giving.

3. They sometimes create the monsters that they ultimately run from. They do this by constantly playing the hero; they also start giving immediately after they meet people, thus perverting the purpose of most of their relationships. In other words, most producers have to repeatedly be delivered from the spirit of sabotage. When their friends, lovers or associates try to be mildly reciprocal, most producers will stop them from doing so. In other words, producers tend to teach people how to take advantage of them.

4. Producers tend to have lifelong friendships with other givers if and when they meet them. Additionally, they make the best of friends!

Producers take mental notes of how or if people reciprocate their giving, and they move accordingly. So, if a producer pays for your lunch a few times, and you never volunteer to pick up the tab, they'll literally stop taking your calls. This isn't to punish you; they do this to teach themselves a lesson because producers can be REALLY hard on themselves; they can even deal with mental torment if they don't set the proper boundaries in place. A producer is almost always happy to be a blessing, but producers often experience their greatest traumas when they come into contact with people who lack gratitude, especially people who are entitled and narcissistic. This is because people who fit this category often open their hearts when they are in a space of giving, and the only thing they are looking to receive in return is the ability to vicariously experience the joy that the taker or receiver is experiencing. However, when things take an unexpected turn, and the receiver begins to complain or ask for more, the producer can go from being a cheerful giver to a frustrated one. This not only ruins the transaction, but because the producer's heart was open in that moment, it can and does set the stage for the giver to be traumatized. This is why you'll find that many givers tend to isolate themselves; they aren't necessarily hiding from people. They are hiding from their own abilities and proclivities. They don't always know how to turn the giver off, so they'd rather stay at home and bless themselves than to do what they're designed to do, and that is to help others. Note: many givers are hoarders, and not like the hoarders you see on television (some of them are); most of them hoard money, their gifts and talents, revelation, etc. This is why producers need regular bouts of deliverance; they also need wise counselors and to be surrounded by other givers. Other facts about givers include:

1. Many givers are abnormally chipper; they are loving people who are known to smile, even when they're sad or depressed.

2. When a giver loses his or her giddiness, that giver often goes to the opposite end of the "happy spectrum." In other words, givers can and do become incredibly bitter if they don't set and enforce boundaries around their giving.

3. Givers tend to attract people who wrestle with jealousy and envy. This is because opposites attract; jealousy is on the far end of the spectrum from giving. Jealousy provokes people to take what they want by force, whereas, the gift of charity (love) compels people to give freely, with no motives attached.

4. Because givers are sensitive, they are easily drained whenever they come in contact with negativity, so if you're a negative person, a giver will intentionally and consistently avoid you.

5. Because many givers or producers are sensitive, they typically have an incredible sense of humor; this is what makes many of them comedians at heart. But this high can be met by extreme lows if they are in the presence of the wrong people.

1 John 4:18 says, "There is no fear in love; but perfect love casteth out fear: because fear hath torment. He that feareth is not made perfect in love." The Greek word for

"perfect" is "teleios," and according to Strong's Concordance, it means "having reached its end, complete, perfect." In short, it means mature love. What if I told you that a large number of producers have attained this level of love? What if I told you that a lot of consumers were gifted with a grace for loving others, but they gave too much to the wrong people, and ended up becoming the very thing that hurt them? You see, whenever you have the gift of charity, what then happens is you will feel an insatiable need to help others and to love on others. You will give people your last, just to help them out, but you soon come to learn that with this particular grace, comes a great deal of heartache. Think about it this way. Imagine if Satan had his own garden; imagine that this garden was similar to the Garden of Eden, but Satan's garden was filled with trees covered in forbidden, ungodly fruits. But there was one tree in the midst of that garden that did not mirror the rest. This was a good tree, and it was covered in good, Godly fruits. The people living in that garden would all take from the evil trees; that is until one day when someone decided to eat from the good tree. Let's call this particular person Hector. After eating one of the fruits, Hector realizes that his breathing has improved, his eyesight has improved and he has more mental clarity. And while he wants to tell everyone else about this particular tree, he also wants to keep it to himself, so every day while everyone else is sleeping, Hector sneaks out to the garden to eat a few of these fruits. Noticing that her husband has been sneaking out, Jennifer decides to follow him. Hector rises from the bed at the first sight of sunlight. He then puts on his favorite pants and quietly slips his feet into his house shoes. With the stealth of a lion, Hector makes his way out of the couple's bedroom, down the hall and finally out through the back door. The alarm system makes a beeping sound anytime a door is opened, so Mary waits for the sound of the beep to slip her shoes on. She then follows her husband to the garden, hiding behind every tree she can find as she trails Hector to his destination. She is alarmed to see Hector making his way towards the one tree that they've been told not to eat from. Hector looks around; the fear in his eyes is evident, but his desire for the forbidden fruits definitely clouds his judgment. Hector pulls down a fruit and admires it before shoving it into his mouth. "What are you doing?" The sound of Jennifer's voice causes a piece of the fruit to lodge itself in Hector's throat. "I can't breathe," he says, pointing at his throat. Realizing that her husband's life is in danger, Jennifer rushes over and performs the Heimlich Maneuver on him. He wheezes three times before the fruit dislodges itself from his throat and flies to the ground. Determined not to let the good fruit go to waste, Hector almost forgets that his wife is behind him. He rushes over to the dislodged fruit, picks it up off the ground and shoves it into his mouth. He closes his eyes as he savors the taste of deliverance. "Hector?!" His wife's voice startles him again. Five minutes later, Hector has convinced his wife to try one of the fruits. She does, and it's the tastiest thing she's ever eaten! "We have to keep this a secret," Hector whispers. And while Jennifer agrees, she's a typical mother. She insists that the couple take some of the fruits home to their children, ages four, seven and ten. The seven-year old and ten-year old recognize the fruits. At first, they whine and complain about their parents' decisions to eat from this particular tree, but after they taste the fruit, they all have a change of heart. The news about the tree spreads quickly after one of Hector and Jennifer's children smuggles one of the fruits into his backpack and takes it to school. Before long, the tree is surrounded by people. And while there are thousands of people taking from that tree, only a few stop to water it or turn its soil. What if I told you that you are that tree? You see, whenever a good person or a giver is discovered by takers, the giver is typically taken advantage of. This sets the stage for trauma, and trauma sets the stage for perversion. The word "pervert" is defined by Oxford Languages as "alter (something) from its original course, meaning, or state to a distortion or corruption of what was first intended." It means that something that should have gone to the right is now moving towards the left; it means that something that was designed to function one way is now malfunctioning. In this case, the giver, because of trauma, becomes a taker. A giver in a world full of takers doesn't stand a chance outside of God. Consequently, to survive, the giver simply stops giving and starts hoarding. They hoard their love, their gifts and their presence. They take the gift of charity and bury it in the backyard of their hearts, and many people who have been graced by God to be a blessing will instead become some of the most manipulative people on the face of this planet. This is because they know how givers think. For example, let's create a common scenario. Your cousin, Sharon, calls and says that she's in town and wants to visit you. At first, you are hesitant to give her your new address, but after a few minutes over the phone, you say to yourself that she can visit, but you're not going to give her anything! After all, Sharon has always been skilled at talking you out of the very things you treasure.

That Saturday afternoon, you receive a knock on the door. It's Sharon, of course, and she doesn't look so happy. She looks sad. You open the door and greet your cousin. "This is my casa!" you shout excitedly. Sharon looks at the ceiling and then looks around the house. "This is nice! You are so blessed! Wait. Why am I surprised? You've always been blessed!" What a kind thing for her to say! You give her a tour of your home, and she compliments your décor and everything about the house. After this, the two of you make your way into the kitchen, and it is in the kitchen that Sharon tells you about her dilemma. "Well, as you know, my mother can be pretty difficult to deal with. Today, she went too far, and to be honest with you, I think that I may have to cut her off. I just discovered three months ago that she is a narcissist, and it all makes sense now! Anyhow, she called Luke, my boyfriend, and asked if I was at his house. He said that I wasn't. She told him that I didn't come home last night. This was a lie! I was in my room the entire time! She didn't even bother to check my bedroom. She simply called out my name a few times, and when I didn't answer her, instead of calling my phone, she called Luke. That woman has always been jealous of me, and I don't understand it!" With those words, Sharon begins to cry. "I just wish that I had a normal mother and a normal family! Sometimes, I feel so alone in this world, and to be honest with you, I'm over it!" Feeling overwhelmed by love and compassion for your cousin, you make your way around the kitchen's island to hug her with all of your might. She cries in your arms as you comfort and reassure her. In that moment, you silently reason with yourself that while Sharon may be toxic, she is a product of her own environment.

Thirty minutes later, Sharon is sitting at the island in your kitchen, smiling and chatting away about her boyfriend. "He's an associate pastor," she says proudly, knowing that these words will impress you given the fact that you are a Christian. "Who would have ever thought that I would be a first lady?" she says bashfully. By the time Sharon leaves, she has an armful of gifts. You've bagged up a lot of your clothes, shoes, jewelry and anything you believe that Sharon would like. And all is well at first. Sharon gets into her car and shouts, "Okay, I'll call you when I get home. Thanks again for everything! I love you, cuzzo!" You blow a kiss at your cousin and watch her back her car out of your driveway. At first, you don't feel anything, but two hours later, regret sets in after you view Sharon's new Facebook post. She posts up several pictures of her standing next to her mother, and while this isn't offensive, it's what her mother is wearing that upsets you. She's wearing one of the hats you gave Sharon and a diamond necklace that you forced yourself to part with. The caption under the photos read, "Like mother, like daughter!" To everyone else, this post seems innocent enough, but to you, it is the evidence that you've just been swindled or taken advantage of by Sharon once again. The women pose for the photos like criminals showing off their loot. You feel disgusted, angry, and most of all, disappointed in yourself. How could you fall for one of Sharon's tricks again? How did you not see this coming? Four years later, you don't have a relationship with a lot of people in your family, and the ones that you do have relationships with, you refuse to let them get close to you. All the same, you won't help others outside of your family because you don't ever want to feel the way you felt when Sharon posted those photos. Consequently, your house is filled with things that you are not using.

The same is true for many who were called to one of the five-fold ministerial offices. They are anointed; they are gifted, but they are also broken. This is why there are many prophets, for example, hiding in most congregations. They sit on the corner seats and at the backs of those churches so that they won't be noticed and so that they can easily escape if they feel seen. Before they understood their wiring or matured in their gifting, they had been hurt, taken advantage of and betrayed. Not wanting to suffer through these events again, they either hide in their homes or in their churches, forgetting Proverbs 18:16, which reads, "A man's gift maketh room for him, and bringeth him before great men." Many of them find themselves attracted to witchcraft because that particular world allows them to be spiritual without any oversight or accountability. In short, trauma makes us forsake one of the many aspects of God, which is JEHOVAH-NISSI (our Banner/Protector) and causes us to forsake Proverbs 3:5-7, which reads, "Trust in the LORD with all thine heart; and lean not unto thine own understanding. In all thy ways acknowledge him, and he shall direct thy paths. Be not wise in thine own eyes: fear the LORD, and depart from evil."

Simplified, if you have this gift, chances are, you need to:
1. Heal.
2. Surround yourself with wise counsel.
3. Ask God for the gift of the discerning of spirits.
4. Be okay with people rejecting you.
5. Stop looking for people to affirm you.
6. Learn to set boundaries.
7. Learn to love some people from a distance.
8. Forgive others.
9. Forgive yourself.
10. Move on!

I have this particular gift and I isolated myself for a long time because of it. I almost felt like a sheep covered in gravy walking amongst a pack of hungry wolves. Nevertheless, once God healed me, strengthened me and educated me, I truly became a new creature in Christ. Now, I have the gift of love, and yes, it is a love that compels me to give, but with this gift, I have the spirit of discernment, the sword of the Spirit, holy boldness, a firm set of boundaries and a willingness to live without people who don't honor the boundaries I've set in place to protect my heart. In other words, one of my superpowers is I don't cling or cleave to toxic people. Instead, the moment I realize that a person is not a good fit for my life, I begin to pray and study that person out of my life. How does this work? It's simple. If you are tolerating broken people, it's because you yourself are broken, plus you have some voids in your life. If you get therapy, buy books and become more intentional about becoming a better version of yourself, those people will fall away like scabs because they won't have any trauma wounds to stick to.

Romantic Warfare

Earlier, we discussed setting standards of communication. This is important because it not only reveals the character and maturity of the people around us, but it purges our intimate spaces of toxic people. You'd be amazed at how so many "good" people were held back in life by toxic people that they simply refused to let go of, mainly because they were related to these people. The graveyard is filled with the bodies of "good" people who could not fathom walking away from the people they called friends and/or family.

- **Luke 12:51-53:** Suppose ye that I am come to give peace on earth? I tell you, Nay; but rather division: For from henceforth there shall be five in one house divided, three against two, and two against three. The father shall be divided against the son, and the son against the father; the mother against the daughter, and the daughter against the mother; the mother in law against her daughter in law, and the daughter in law against her mother in law.
- **Matthew 10:37:** He that loveth father or mother more than me is not worthy of me: and he that loveth son or daughter more than me is not worthy of me.
- **1 Corinthians 15:33:** Be not deceived: evil communications corrupt good manners.

In truth, we'd all love to believe that we can bring whomever we want into our intimate spaces, and this couldn't be further from the truth than it already is. The people who have intimate access to you will create soul ties with you, and these soul ties become yokes when they're ungodly. But let's visit the topic of soul ties, because believe it or not, there are still people on the face of this Earth who do not believe that they exist. Let's look at a few scriptures:

- **1 Samuel 18:1:** And it came to pass, when he had made an end of speaking unto Saul, that the soul of Jonathan was knit with the soul of David, and Jonathan loved him as his own soul.
- **1 Corinthians 6:15-17:** Know ye not that your bodies are the members of Christ? Shall I then take the members of Christ, and make them the members of an harlot? God forbid. What? know ye not that he which is joined to an harlot is one body? for two, saith he, shall be one flesh. But he that is joined unto the Lord is one spirit.

Believe it or not, sometimes, we can serve as evil communicators in another person's life. Later on in this book, we will discuss this. Most of us want mentors and leaders who we can talk to about our problems in hopes that they can give us some advice and coach us through the tough patches in our lives. And while this is great, let me share three issues with you that keep a lot of people from getting or maintaining access to the wise counselors that the Bible instructs us to have.

1. **Entitlement:** Some people genuinely feel entitled to the time and resources of other people. They are especially demanding of Christian leaders. I remember my former pastor addressing this with the congregation. He mentioned how so many pastors had allowed their congregants to destroy their marriages by being entitled and demanding of their time. He then told us that whenever he is home with his wife and children, that's family time. And during this time, he doesn't answer calls, nor does he do house calls. I was proud to know that he had boundaries in place to protect himself and his family.

2. **Lack of Honor:** Every curse that has ever found its way into this Earth has come because of dishonor. Think about it! Lucifer sinned against God because of his dishonor towards God. He wanted to make himself equal with God; he wanted to split God's Kingdom in half. What exactly is honor? Oxford Languages defines it as "high respect; great esteem." The Greek word for "honor" is "timaō" and, according to Thayer's Greek Lexicon, it means "to estimate, fix the value." It means to value someone. Honor shows up in how you treat a person, how you respect that person's time and in the fact that you don't feel entitled to that person's time. (If you want to learn more about honor intelligence, be sure to purchase the book I wrote with my pastor, Apostle Bryan Meadows, entitled *Honor Intelligence*. You can find it on Amazon.)

3. **Lack of Relational Intelligence:** A lot of people were raised to see everyone as equal to themselves, including other adults. When I was growing up, my siblings and I were required to say "ma'am" and "sir" to our elders. There were certain things that we could not say to adults and authority figures. My mother demonstrated this very well. Even though she was an adult, she still referred to her elders and anyone in authority (even people younger than herself) as "ma'am" and "sir." She didn't seek to make herself equal to them or to lord herself over them. She recognized rank and acted accordingly. Nowadays, people not only lack relational acuity, but the spirit of offense is running rampant! Consequently, the stench of dishonor rises up to Heaven, causing the Heavens to shut over so many people's lives.

There's a theory I have called the Grenade Effect, but I liken it to chemicals. What this looks like is—a person will see a leader that he or she wants to connect with. Get this—there are many ways to connect with people, but whenever you come across leaders, don't always assume that you need a friendship connection with them. If you need therapy, hire a therapist. If you need mentoring, hire a mentor. If you need a life coach, hire one. If you need a pastor, go and submit to one, but don't always assume that they owe you their friendship and their time. Sure, your pastor could give you a little therapy here and there, but always keep in mind that your pastor is not your therapist. I say this because a lot of people have walked away from the church offended because they genuinely felt hurt by the fact that their pastors had boundaries that kept them from accessing them the way they wanted to. They didn't realize that they could not handle the level of access that they were lusting after. This is where the Grenade Effect comes in. What is the Grenade Effect? Let's look at an example. Morgan has been in search of a good church home ever since she stormed out of her last church. At her last church, she'd volunteered, bought presents for her pastor and even promoted the church on her radio station. Nevertheless, Morgan always felt rejected by her pastor. Sure, he'd been nice to her, but every time she logged onto social media, she would see pictures of him hanging out with other members, whereas she only saw him on Sundays and Tuesdays. After a new member posted pictures of herself and the pastor out at a race car track, Morgan found herself overcome with hurt, anger and confusion. So, without warning, she simply stopped attending services, but she didn't want to leave without first shooting an arrow at her pastor to let him know just what she thought about him. So, one day, she sent him a long email, accusing him of favoritism. In the email, she listed all of the things she'd done for the church and all the seeds she'd sown, and then she bid the pastor farewell. "I'm washing my hands and dusting off my feet," she said in her last line. "Goodbye and good riddance! I hope you learn to stop hurting people!" For more than a week, Morgan checked her email, hoping that her now former pastor would respond and explain himself to her, but this didn't happen. This caused her to become even more offended, so she talked about the incident on her radio station. A lot of unbelievers and immature Christians responded in the chat with words like, "That's why I don't go to church" or "That's why I don't believe in organized religion." In other words, she led many people astray.

After watching a few church services online, Morgan found a church she felt would be perfect for her. It was smaller than the one she'd left, so she reasoned within herself that maybe she wouldn't have to compete with so many people for the pastor's attention. Her new pastor was an older man with a slight limp. Morgan joined the church after visiting two times, and like she'd done at her former church, she started sowing seeds, volunteering and being present every time the church's doors opened. And one day, it all paid off. One of the leaders at the church spoke with Morgan about helping the pastor to establish his own podcast, and Morgan happily agreed to do it. "Pastor Mark definitely needs one," she said. "His voice needs to go to the nations!" Two weeks later, Morgan found herself at a restaurant with her pastor, talking about her idea for his new podcast. She felt seen, heard and appreciated; she was beside herself with joy. A month later, Pastor Mark's new podcast hit the internet, and Morgan insisted that he have a website built for himself, and she paid one of her nephews to create it. Everything was going great! She was working with the pastor a lot, helping the church to grow its online presence.

One day, Pastor Mark went to his office, thinking that no one else was at the church. He'd just had another fight with his wife, so he'd gone to the church to get some fresh air and so that he could have a more peaceful atmosphere to write his Sunday sermon in. Morgan had used her key to let herself in just thirty minutes prior to the pastor's arrival. She'd stopped by the church to vacuum the sanctuary. The sound of the door opening startled Morgan so much that she'd cursed out loud. "I'm so sorry," she said when she saw her pastor's face. "I thought I was here alone." Pastor Mark was equally startled. "Yeah, me too," he said as he closed the door. "What are you doing here?" Morgan pulled the plug of the vacuum cleaner out of the wall and started wrapping it up. "I was just leaving," she said. "I stopped by to vacuum the church, but I just finished. What are you doing here?" Pastor Mark diverted his eyes to look at the sanctuary. "Well, it looks good in there. Thank you very much! I just decided to stop by to get some fresh air." Morgan could tell that something was wrong with her pastor. All the same, she didn't want to pry too much because she didn't want to come off as nosy. "Okay," she said. "Wait. Pastor, what's wrong?" Pastor Mark searched her eyes; he began to weigh the situation. Would it be a good idea to confide in Morgan? Without warning, he blurted it all out. "Mi-Mi, I mean Pastor Michelle can be difficult to live with at times. She's been whining and complaining all day about everything from the empty refrigerator to the broken garage door. That woman called me prideful when I said that I didn't need to hire anyone to fix anything. I'll fix it when I get ready! But, she wouldn't stop talking, so I saw myself out. God gave me a way of escape called a front door, so I took it," he said as he chuckled and tried to make light of the event. Morgan cleared her throat. "Well, it sounds to me like you have a lot on your plate. Just remember—happy wife, happy life!" Regretting everything he'd just said, Pastor Mark apologized. "I'm sorry. I shouldn't have dumped all that on you," he said. "But thank you for all that you do. I'll be in my office." With those words, he began to walk towards his office. "Wait!" Morgan shouted. "My brother-in-law is a handyman. I could have him stop by and fix whatever needs to be fixed. No charge!"

Three weeks later, Morgan found herself getting the rebuke of her life from Pastor Mark. He'd preached that day, and after service, he'd heard a knock on his office door. "Who is it?" he asked. That's when Morgan let herself in. "Pastor, can I speak with you real quick?" she'd asked. Pastor Mark finished buttoning up his shirt. "Yes ma'am, but next time, don't barge in like that. Wait for me to invite you in." Morgan nodded her head. "Okay, I'll take heed next time. Pastor, I have something to say, and I hope you don't take offense to this, but ..." With those words, Morgan began to search her pastor's eyes. Would he be offended or would he listen to what she believed to be wise counsel? Seeing that he had not broken eye contact with her, she continued. "Maybe, you should consider ironing your clothes before you leave the house, or you can bring them to the church and I'll iron them," she said. "Today, I couldn't help but notice the wrinkles, and I'm a perfectionist, so...." Before she could finish, Pastor Mark cut her off. "Now Morgan, that's not okay! You have to learn to respect boundaries, young lady. If I needed someone to iron my clothes, I'd ask my wife. All the same, this is the third time this week that you've tried to insert yourself into something that does not concern you. Tuesday, you asked me if my wife had stopped nagging me, and I let that go when I should've corrected you then! Thursday, you stopped by the church just to tell me that I needed to enunciate my words better. Who does that?! Remember, I'm your pastor, not your friend." Offended, Morgan stormed out of the pastor's office and out of the church. Two weeks later, she recorded another podcast; this time, attempting to expose her newly former pastor. "How can he pastor a church when he can't even fix his own house?" she shouted over the radio.

This is a growing scenario in today's western church. Morgan wanted intimate access to her leaders, and she used bait to get it. Understand that any seed that has motives attached to it is not a seed, it's bait! When her first pastor did not take the bait, she became so offended that she not only left the church, she decided to blast him on her show. Thankfully, she hadn't had any intimate access to him, therefore, she could only blast surface-level information and assumptions. What if I told you that her first pastor wasn't just hanging out with the people, they were having meetings? All meetings don't have to be in an office! Every person the pastor hung out with was volunteering with the ministry in some form or fashion, and having a meeting with the pastor is not a reward for volunteering. Typically, leaders set up meetings to discuss their plans with the people who can help to carry them out. But Morgan didn't see it this way. She tried to buy or lease access to her pastor, and after this failed, she left her church in search of a pastor that she could soul-tie herself to and potentially control. This is demonic behavior! And not long after she'd left her first church, she'd met Pastor Mark, and get this—Pastor Mark's church was smaller, so he had more needs that were unmet than her former pastor. Morgan saw this as an opportunity to walk alongside her pastor, but the minute she saw his humanity, she became too familiar. This always sets the stage for the spirit of control to enter the picture. Consequently, she started behaving in a dishonorable fashion. This is the Grenade Effect. How does this work? Whenever I was introduced to this concept by the Lord, I saw a vision of a person being rolled into a church like a hand grenade. On the surface, the person's intentions are cloudy, but not necessarily malicious. What do I mean by cloudy? What makes it impure is that the person, in many cases, may want power, positions, and the privileges that come with them both. And the person is not willing to go through the normal chain of command to acquire these things. "Verily, verily, I say unto you, He that entereth not by the door into the sheepfold, but climbeth up some other way, the same is a thief and a robber" (John 10:1). It all starts with the spirit of rejection. If the person is not healed from rejection and delivered from the spirit of rejection, that demon will fill the individual's mind with delusions of success, power and grandeur. The person in question will then begin to use flattery and gifts in his or her attempt to gain intimate access to a leader, thus skipping Circles 5, 4, and 3 in an attempt to get to Circles 1 or 2. If and when the individual succeeds, that person will then begin the process of familiarizing herself (let's say it was a woman) with the leader. The problem with this is, while her intentions are pure, Satan has planted some evil in her that she may not be aware of, and he knows that the pastor's wiring will trigger an explosion. This is why I call it the Grenade Effect. This is exactly what Saul did to David. Let's look at the story.

- **1 Samuel 18:20-21:** And Michal Saul's daughter loved David: and they told Saul, and the thing pleased him. And Saul said, I will give him her, that she may be a snare to him, and that the hand of the Philistines may be against him. Wherefore Saul said to David, Thou shalt this day be my son in law in the one of the twain.

- **2 Samuel 6:16-23:** And as the ark of the LORD came into the city of David, Michal Saul's daughter looked through a window, and saw king David leaping and dancing before the LORD; and she despised him in her heart. And they brought in the ark of the LORD, and set it in his place, in the midst of the tabernacle that David had pitched for it: and David offered burnt offerings and peace offerings before the LORD. And as soon as David had made an end of offering burnt offerings and peace offerings, he blessed the people in the name of the LORD of hosts. And he dealt among all the people, even among the whole multitude of Israel, as well to the women as men, to every one a cake of bread, and a good piece of flesh, and a flagon of wine. So all the people departed every one to his house. Then David returned to bless his household. And Michal the daughter of Saul came out to meet David, and said, How glorious was the king of Israel to day, who uncovered himself to day in the eyes of the handmaids of his servants, as one of the vain fellows shamelessly uncovereth himself! And David said unto Michal, It was before the LORD, which chose me before thy father, and before all his house, to appoint me ruler over the people of the LORD, over Israel: therefore will I play before the LORD. And I will yet be more vile than thus, and will be base in mine own sight: and of the maidservants which thou hast spoken of, of them shall I be had in honour. Therefore Michal the daughter of Saul had no child unto the day of her death.

Notice here that Michal had no idea that she was bait; she was a grenade rolled into David's life designed to expose him to his enemy. This is why whenever I'm counseling people who are dealing with broken hearts, I typically tell them that the people who broke their hearts likely didn't have malicious intent when they met them. Their motives, while murky, were not that bad. But Satan knew what was in them, and he also knew that everyone he sent into your life had what can best be described as a certain chemical makeup. Their chemical makeup and your chemical makeup would only cause you both to spiritually combust. This is to say that if you are single and you decide that you like someone, or that person decides that he or she likes you, Satan will attempt to bring the both of you together if one or both of you are broken, toxic and in need of deliverance. Understand this—your brokenness may not look like their brokenness. Yours may manifest as you being super giving, extremely trustworthy and by you not guarding your heart, thus causing you to move your new romantic interest from Circle 5 to Circle 1 within a matter of days or weeks. Your new boyfriend or girlfriend's brokenness may manifest as love-bombing, obsession and an overwhelming desire to be with you every second of the day. This will likely be followed by fear, insecurity and suspicion, all of which will ultimately be followed by jealousy, rage, abuse and maybe even murder. This is called romantic warfare. It starts with America's favorite demons: lust, obsession and fornication; these three come to open the door for the rest of their demonic party. After a soul tie has been formed, the rest of the demonic guests will arrive. This is when demons start the process of digging. Digging is demonic activity where demons cause people to help them dig holes in the souls of other people through an event called trauma. In the realm of the spirit, this looks like a wrecking ball hitting the heart. The ditches that are created become cave-like structures that demons house themselves in. This is why deliverance, while needed, does not complete a process. Instead, deliverance casts the demon out of the darkness, but it does not turn on the lights or heal the wounds.

Romantic warfare involves love-bombing, cloud nine, dishonor and disobedience. First and foremost, what is love-bombing? The following information was taken from Dictionary.com:

> "Love bombing is the practice of showing a person excessive affection and attention as a way of manipulating them in a relationship.

The term is most commonly used in a negative way in the context of individuals who use it on romantic partners (or desired romantic partners) or cult members who use it as a recruitment technique. Love bombing typically takes the form of showering a person with a combination of seemingly genuine expressions of love or attention, such as excessive praise, gifts, and grand gestures. In love bombing, this behavior goes beyond the heightened level of attention that can be common at the beginning of relationships.

It is thought to be part of a pattern of emotionally abusive behavior in which it is done to socially isolate and control a person by making them emotionally and socially dependent on the manipulator. After the manipulator gains a level of control, they often become distant and begin to engage in other forms of emotional abuse, such as gaslighting" (Source: Dictionary.com/Love Bombing/What is Love Bombing?)

Think of it as an actual war. During the love-bombing phase, one or both parties is lifted to what we commonly refer to as "cloud nine." This phrase is normally used to describe elation, happiness and a state of total euphoria. The problem with cloud nine is it's all vapor; it's not real. A healthy relationship has substance. This is why we need faith to please God (see Hebrews 11:6), and faith is the SUBSTANCE of things hoped for and the EVIDENCE of things not seen (see Hebrews 11:1). The substance we need to build healthy, Godly relationships, on the other hand, is information; it's what we've come to know, appreciate and understand about one another. Howbeit, in the building of a toxic relationship, this particular step is skipped. Sure, the people share some surface-level information about themselves with one another, along with a few intimate facts, but they genuinely do not know one another. This is what allows them to float to cloud nine. Cloud nine simply means that one or both of the parties involved is not sober; they are under the influence of an imagination or belief. "Be sober, be vigilant; because your adversary the devil, as a roaring lion, walketh about, seeking whom he may devour" (1 Peter 5:8). "Casting down imaginations, and every high thing that exalteth itself against the knowledge of God, and bringing into captivity every thought to the obedience of Christ" (2 Corinthians 10:5). When at least one of the people involved in the relationship begins to sober up, that person begins to sink; they typically sink into a dimension called insecurity. Insecurity has doors that lead to sex outside of marriage. It does this by causing one of the parties involved in the relationship to start fearing that the other person may become bored or feel unappreciated. Consequently, the insecure individual will attempt to "spice things up" by touching on the other person, kissing the other person, repeatedly love-bombing the other person, and then sexting the other person (if allowed). This allows the party of two to ascend back to cloud nine or, better yet, get high off the lies they've told themselves and the lies they've told one another. The purpose of these lies is to replace the substance that the relationship needs to survive. Please note that this is where dishonor and disobedience both enter the equation, thus giving Satan the deed to this relationship. It's dishonor because the woman typically carries her father's last name. The word "maiden" means "virgin," so a woman's maiden name is her virgin name. It is (or should be) her father's name, paternal grandfather's name and paternal great-grandfather's name. Any time a woman has sex while wearing her father's name, both her and the man she's engaging in sexual activity enter a realm called dishonor. All the same, sex outside of marriage is rebellion, and the Bible tells us that rebellion is as the sin of witchcraft (see 1 Samuel 15:23). Once Satan has full rights to the relationship, he begins to toy with the parties involved. He does this by inundating one of the lovers with negative thoughts about the other lover. Consequently, that individual begins to sober up, and after a while, he or she will develop immunity to the other person's words, sex and gifts. You would think that the newly sober lover would end the relationship in that moment, but in many cases, the breakup happens months or even years after the individual has sobered up. The person may stick around because of a benefit that he or she is extracting from the relationship or, in most cases, because he or she may fear losing the other person. It doesn't make sense to those of us who are of a sound mind, but the way this works is—the partially sober individual will, in many cases, enjoy the worship that he or she receives from the other party. In most cases, it is the guy who sobers up first. When this happens, he is completely cognizant of the fact that he does not love the woman he's entertaining, but he may begin to objectify her. In other words, she then becomes a possession of his. Note: men aren't the only ones who do this! Many women do this to men as well, especially after they've had children with them. The guys in question then become the fathers of their children and sources of income. This is objectification! This is where the wrecking ball of trauma comes out. The parties will traumatize one another until Satan tires of toying around with them. Again, when he has the deed to a relationship, he gets to determine the direction of that relationship by determining the weather of that relationship.

Once the relationship ends, both parties are normally in need of therapy and deliverance, but how many people in the western world seek therapy after a failed relationship? The majority of people don't! And get this—those newly formed voids (trauma wounds) have gravitational pulls. Again, these pulls or forces are called attraction. The problem is that while this hole in the soul grows, causing the person to become more anxious for a relationship, that person's attraction to a certain type also grows because the void will oftentimes take the shape of the demon that inhabits it. So, what will you be attracted to? A familiar spirit! We call this our "type." For example, you may hear a friend of yours saying, "Girl, he's not my type!" This is why we tend to date the same demon in a different person; that is until we go through the healing and deliverance process and begin to fill ourselves with revelation. The average person will repeatedly fall under the spell of what the world calls "falling in love," not realizing that the sweaty palms, racing heart and butterflies in the stomach feelings are all the heart's way of warning us that it has been hijacked.

To avoid romantic warfare, follow these steps:

1. Every new love interest that you meet must enter into your life through Circle 5 and GRADUALLY make his or her way towards your heart.

2. Information! Get information! Learn about the person, and don't allow the individual to love-bomb you or rush his or her way into your intimate space.

3. Heal! If you don't heal before dating or courting, you will almost always attract the very spirit that hurt you in the first place. This process is called reconciliation or, better yet, the return of the unclean spirit (see Matthew 12:43-45).

4. If the person does not love the Lord, that person cannot and will not love you, after all, God is love.

5. Keep sin out of your relationship; this way, God will possess the deed to it.

6. Do not be unequally yoked with unbelievers (see 2 Corinthians 6:14).

7. Utilize your multitude of counselors; ask questions, and apply what you've learned.

8. Do not envy anyone else's relationship. This will only cause you to rush the one you're in.

9. If your love interest tries to pull away, let him or her go! When people attempt to pull away after you've done all the right things, the problem typically is they don't know how to have civil, Godly relationships. All the same, if they are in need of deliverance, you have not given their demons the offering they need to legalize themselves in your life. Consequently, James 4:7 comes into play; it reads, "Submit yourselves therefore to God.

Resist the devil, and he will flee from you." Not only will the devil flee from you whenever you submit yourself to God, but folks who have the devil in them will also run. This is why I said do not chase them!

10. Keep prayer at the forefront, and refuse to make an idol out of marriage, out of yourself and out of your love interest.

GOOD INTENTIONS, BAD HEARTS

In the previous chapter, we briefly spoke about people having good intentions with bad hearts. What this means is—a lot of the people you'll meet over the course of your life will genuinely want to be your friend, your lover or fill some role in your life, and many of these people will have good intentions. Nevertheless, your chemical makeup (spiritually speaking) will trigger their chemical makeup, causing sparks to fly. In other words, iron sharpens iron, but what happens if you are as tough as metal, but the person you're attempting to sharpen is as fragile as aluminum foil? Why is this important? Because it's easy for people with good intentions to convince you that their plans for you are good and pure because they themselves are convinced that their intentions are good. This is why the Bible tells us to test the spirits of the people we come in contact with (see 1 John 4:1) and to examine their fruits (see Matthew 7:16). But before we delve into this, let's talk about closing doors on expired and ungodly relationships.

It is not uncommon for me to get this question— "I have someone in my life who God has been telling me to separate myself from. How do I go about doing this? Should I just cut her off?" I remember having this question many times myself. God kept sending prophets and prophetic people to warn me about people who were in my life. Because I am an introvert, I would almost always have one or two people in my intimate circle at any given time, so it wasn't hard to figure out who God wanted me to remove. The hard part was figuring out how to remove the individual in question. I remember being bound by toxic loyalty. This is when you are so grateful for a person's presence, tenure and all that the person has done for you that you refuse to let him or her go, despite all of the warnings you receive. In this, you prioritize your loyalty to them over your loyalty to God and your God-given assignment. So, I asked the Lord to help me to exit any and every relationship that He didn't want me in, and He did just that—just not the way I expected. What I learned in this is—you have to die your way out of an ungodly relationship and friendship. And note that by "ungodly," I mean:

1. Demonic Relationships.
2. Expired Relationships.
3. Ungodly Soul Ties.
4. Co-Dependent Relationships.
5. Trauma Bonded Relationships.
6. Toxic Relationships.
7. Idolatrous Relationships.

How do you die your way out of a relationship? It's simple:

1. Change your mind.
2. Change your conversations. Never engage in gossip or slander.
3. Use your voice. Stop being passive!
4. Embrace your God-given identity and assignment.
5. Mature in Christ.
6. Heal.
7. Pray instead of complaining.

8. Practice and master honoring others. Most ungodly soul ties are created in the realm of dishonor.
9. Encourage others, instead of belittling them.
10. Forgive.
11. Study the Word of God daily.
12. Don't listen to anyone brag about their sins and don't let them sin in your presence; create boundaries and enforce them.
13. Be okay with being alone for a few seasons if you have to. Don't keep people around just because you're bored or you're afraid to walk alone. Remember, God Is with you!
14. Don't let anyone muzzle you.

Let's talk about expired relationships. When a relationship expires, God exits the relationship, but He remains with the people in the relationship (if they are believers). God is Light; this means that He is wrapped in glory, and light, of course, represents revelation. So, when God isn't present in a relationship, the relationship then becomes dark, demonic and toxic. When there is no revelation going forth, the conversations produced will oftentimes be laced with gossip, slander, misinformation and perversion. Keep in mind that demonic relationships work against you, not for you. Expired relationships are hard to walk away from because they once served a purpose, and the thought of walking away from people who once helped or encouraged us feels like betrayal. No sane person wants to betray another person! But what if I told you that God doesn't always require you to walk away from people? He wants you to:

1. Change your mind. You do this by changing what goes in through your ear gates and eye gates.
2. Place that individual in the right circle. For example, your best friend may no longer qualify for Circle 1 because she's heading in a different direction than you. So, you'd move her to Circle 2, and then Circle 3, 4 and 5 (if necessary). Most of the time, you won't have to do so much moving. If she's no good for you, she will more than likely walk away once she loses intimate access to you.

One of the reasons that God moves people around in your life is so that He can activate your voice. This is to say that expired, toxic and demonic relationships often serve one purpose in a person's life, and that is to muzzle that person. Understand that you are here for a reason. You have an assignment on Earth, and it is the heart and the will of God to position you in the right relationships so that you can fulfill that assignment, but again, whenever you have the wrong people too close to you, they will almost always act as muzzles. For example, one of the ways I can tell if a person is not mature enough for my intimate circle is by paying attention to how they manage my voice.

- Can I be myself with the individual, or do I have to suppress my voice or any part of my personality to keep the individual from being offended?
- Is the person easily offended?
- How does the person handle offense?
- Does the person often misunderstand what I'm saying?
- Do I have to explain in detail a lot of what I share

with that person?

- Do I have to dumb myself down to host that person's presence in my life?
- Whenever I speak or teach, do I feel pressured to mind what I say out of fear of offending the person?
- Do I feel guilty or do I feel like I have to repent immediately after speaking with that person?
- Is the person competitive?

The goal is to be on the lookout for the spirit of control. Believe it or not, this spirit is prevalent today, and it seeks to silence God's people by using the spirit of offense as a muzzle. For example, before I wrote my first book or recorded my first video, I used to write for a publication called Examiner. I took on the role of the Jackson, Mississippi Christian Living Examiner. I was excited when I started writing for the publication because it was a national magazine with millions of subscribers. When I started writing for them, I wrote mainly about relationships, purpose and demonology. Even though I didn't know a lot about demonology, what I did know surely attracted a crowd of curious people. One of those people was a young lady who'd read an article I'd written about the Jezebel spirit. Without going too deep into the matter, she'd reached out to me after reading the article because she said her mother was bound by that particular spirit. I didn't have any boundaries in place, so after chatting with her a few times, I agreed to speak with her over the phone. We ended up having a four-hour conversation, and at the end of that conversation, she'd managed to jump from

Circle 6 (meaning she was a stranger) to Circle 2. Within two weeks, she was in Circle 1 because I spoke with her everyday, and I overshared my life with her because she'd overshared her life with me. In other words, I was still bound by toxic reciprocity, meaning I felt the need to do and say whatever someone did and said to me. So, when she said, "I feel like you're my best friend," I echoed her words back to her. Don't get me wrong—she wasn't a bad person at all. The problem was that she wasn't mature enough to walk so close to me, and I wasn't mature enough to realize this. A few months later, I received an inbox or a text message from her inquiring about an article I'd just posted. She asked me if the article was about her. Thankfully, she was friendly about it, and I was able to diffuse her suspicions. Nevertheless, this hadn't been the first time I'd had someone asking or accusing me of writing an article about them. On one instance, I'd received an inbox message on Facebook from a woman who believed the article I'd just posted was about her. The problem with this logic is—I didn't know the woman—at all! I had never spoken with the woman, and I'm not sure how she got on my friends' list. Nevertheless, the woman was insistent that I'd read one of her Facebook posts and I'd written my article in response to what she'd posted. This wasn't true, of course. I don't think I'd ever visited her page, but I soon learned that Satan will harass people with the following thoughts:

- "They're talking about you."
- "They listened to what somebody said about you!"
- "Their posts are about you!"
- "They judged you without knowing you. You're a

good person, but they were too lazy to find this out for themselves!"

- "They're jealous of you!"
- "They're intimidated by you!"
- "They're laughing at you!"

These thoughts are rarely, if ever, true. Nevertheless, people believe what pops up in their minds, and they don't bother trying to test the spirits behind those thoughts or communicate with the person or people they're offended with. Instead, they draft up a bunch of theories in their minds, and then they respond accordingly. Again, I was grateful that the young lady I'd befriended was reaching out to me to see if I'd posted about her, rather than attempting to punish me, which is something I'd experienced a few other people do. So, I thanked her for reaching out to me, and I explained to her what had motivated me to write the article. I hadn't thought about her a single time while writing. All the same, I explained to her that I am not passive-aggressive; I don't use my platform to attack, communicate with or belittle people. Howbeit, the damage was already done (to my heart, that is), and truth be told, it wasn't entirely her fault. I'd had to explain myself one too many times, and unfortunately, even though I had a mentor at that time, he wasn't an influencer, so he couldn't mentor me in that area of my life. Because of this, I began to silently question myself. Was I writing posts and articles about people after all? What if I was doing this subconsciously, not realizing that I had been motivated by a conversation I'd had earlier? In many instances, I knew that the articles were not conversations that had somehow resurfaced because I'd been planning to write them, I'd already written them or I was in the process of writing them before the person reached out to me! It took me some time before I realized that Satan was using people to muzzle me. I soon found myself overthinking everything I wrote. I would literally spend hours writing an article, only to deal with harassing thoughts that sounded like:

- "Oh, don't you remember that you discussed something similar with (insert name here) last week?! She's going to think you're talking about her! You'd better not post this article!"
- "(Insert name here) posted a status on this same subject! She's going to think you're talking about her! You better write another article!"
- "(Insert name here) suffers from that issue! If you post that article, she's going to swear you're posting about her!"

I'm sure I deleted at least 35 articles because I kept overthinking, not realizing that I was in the center of warfare. Satan was trying to muzzle me, and he was doing a great job at it! As an influencer, one of my greatest frustrations has been in the fact that a lot of people will fight, claw and try to lie their way into Circle 1 of our lives, but they can't even handle Circles 3 or 4! If they get too close to us, Satan torments them with thoughts of us talking, teaching or preaching about them, thoughts of us thinking we're too good for them or thoughts of us abandoning them whenever we find "better friends." He does this so that they can attempt to silence us, control our voices or make us feel guilty whenever we start to ascend in the areas that we're called to. All the same, if the influencer doesn't allow them to get close, the spirit of rejection torments them. It tells them that we're judging them, we think we're too good for them or someone has said something to us about them. In other words, Satan uses good people or people with good intentions to do bad things. Ask any influencer and they will tell you stories upon stories of people who've pushed, shoved and fought for a place in their lives, only to get close to them and start complaining about the things they routinely said, the lessons they taught, their mannerisms and the way they speak. This gives weight to that old adage "darned if you do, darned if you don't." This is the reality of an influencer, but it's also your reality, believe it or not. How so? Sometimes, people's demons are attracted to your demons, or their demons can be attracted to your anointing. Either way, they will passionately attempt to build a relationship with you, and then get offended if you don't reciprocate their efforts.

Human muzzles are oftentimes people with good intentions, but behind those intentions and wide smiles are motives. And get this—their motives are not always impure. For example, a woman may decide that she wants to walk closely with you because of your relationship with God. She may say in her heart, "If I had a friend like her (or him), I'd be a better person. I know she'd hold me accountable, and I'd go to church more." Her motives are pure, but her heart is not in good shape. So, the best place for her in your life is Circle 5 (for starters). This means that you can mentor her, either directly or indirectly. Nevertheless, because of her immaturity, she will try to find a way to get into your intimate circle, not realizing that she's not mature enough to handle being stretched or being corrected. Additionally, when we bring people close to our hearts who are not mature or healthy enough to have that level of access, they will oftentimes endure a lot of warfare, because get this—when Satan can't get to you through you, he'll try to get to you through someone close to you. In other words, Satan will do one or two things to the aforementioned woman (if she doesn't humble herself and refuses to be patient with God):

1. Cause her to feel offended when you place boundaries in front of her. Some people take this really hard because the enemy keeps reminding them that their intentions were good. He will then torment her with negative thoughts about you. These thoughts usually provoke the spirit of rejection to rise up, causing her to feel misunderstood, unwanted and misjudged.

2. Cause her to minimize and then muzzle you if she gets the role and/or position that she wants. He'll do this by making her share or overshare her life with you, and then he'll torment her with the thought of you sharing that information with someone else (gossip), you judging her because of what she's shared with you or you disassociating yourself from her because of what she's told you. And if you're a leader, Satan will repeatedly tell her that your messages and posts are about her. Again,

the goal is to get her to become offended and muzzle you.

This would mean that the only way you could entertain her in Circle 1 would be if you allowed her to passively control and muzzle you. Sadly enough, there are a lot of leaders and people out there who are being muzzled by the spirits of control, offense and witchcraft, and most of the people Satan uses to muzzle them have good intentions, but their hearts are not good.

Let's take another stab at what this looks like romantically. Jamal is a kindhearted man who is devoted to his three children. All of the children have different mothers, but regardless of this fact, Jamal is very much present in their lives and he happily supports them financially. Jamal has a friend named Kendra, and the two of them have been friends for a little more than eight years. Jamal's oldest son is seven-years old, and his youngest son is two-years old. His middle child, who's also a boy, is four-years old. This means that Kendra has been in Jamal's life since before he became a father. And while the two are close friends, they've never dated, kissed or had sex. This is because Kendra drew a boundary almost immediately after meeting Jamal. You see, the two met at a self-defense class. Jamal was the instructor and Kendra was one of the students. What made her stand out was the fact that she was attentive, determined and she learned faster than the other women, many of whom had only registered for the class because of their attraction to Jamal. After class was over one day, Kendra had stayed behind looking for her keys. This caused Jamal to have to keep the gym open a little longer, and while he was frustrated, he didn't want to rush the beautiful Kendra out of the space. They ended up finding Kendra's keys an hour later. Someone had intentionally placed them in an overhead bin, and Jamal immediately knew who to suspect of this wicked deed. Two of the women who'd joined the class (Pamela and Ivy) were amongst the category of women who'd joined the class to flirt with Jamal. When they'd noticed how Jamal looked at Kendra, the two friends had gotten together and decided to sabotage the woman they saw as a threat. Jamal managed to thwart their efforts one day when he saw them placing a lizard in Kendra's bag. When he'd confronted the women, they claimed that it was all a joke. Nevertheless, Jamal knew that it wasn't a joke because he'd seen the way the women looked at Kendra. All the same, Pamela had once stayed behind to tell Jamal how handsome he was and to warn him about her friend, Ivy, who she said was bipolar. This is to say that Jamal knew that the women were guilty of hiding Kendra's keys. The time they took to look for those keys had worked out in their favor. They'd joked, shared a little of their stories with one another and encouraged one another. And now, eight years later, they were still pretty good friends. Despite Jamal's efforts to woo her, Kendra had always insisted on remaining friends with Jamal because she didn't see Jamal as a one-woman man. All the same, Jamal had helped Kendra out a lot over the years. He'd even purchased her a used car when she'd returned to college to get her Master's degree! So, by all accounts and purposes, Jamal appeared to be perfect for Kendra, and the people around them secretly wished the two would stop playing games with one another and just start dating! And one day, their wish materialized!

It had been four months since Kendra's breakup from her long-term boyfriend, Terrence, and she'd decided to hang out with Jamal for his 32nd birthday since he didn't have any plans. Kendra ended up taking Jamal to his favorite restaurant, and while they were there, Jamal professed his love for his best friend. Kendra wasn't shocked at the fact that Jamal wanted to be in a relationship with her, after all, he'd been flirting with her since the moment they'd laid eyes on one another, but this night felt different. Maybe, it was because her heart wasn't fully healed from her breakup, or maybe it was the fact that Jamal had shed a few tears while detailing to Kendra just how much he loved her. Either way, that night, Kendra saw Jamal in a different light. "Okay," she said. "I'll date you, but ..." Before she could finish, Jamal clinched his fist and drew his arm towards his chest in a celebratory fashion. "Yes!" he exclaimed as a few of the patrons in the restaurant turned around to see the man who'd dare disturb such an ambient atmosphere. "But," Kendra said pointing at her eyes, and then at Jamal's eyes, indicating that she wanted eye contact. "But, Jamal. No funny business! I love you as a friend, and I'd rather keep you as a friend than lose you as a boyfriend." Jamal was convinced that he wouldn't betray Kendra, after all, they'd been friends for well over eight years and Kendra was the girl of his dreams.

The first four months of their relationship were a struggle. While they now labeled one another as "boyfriend" and "girlfriend," Jamal felt like Kendra was still treating him as a friend. They hadn't shared their first kiss, they rarely held hands when they hung out and Kendra still insisted that Jamal remain in the living room when visiting her. She didn't visit him because he lived with his younger brother. This all changed when the couple hung out one night at a beach near Kendra's apartment. They'd held hands and walked on the beach as the waves swept across their bare feet. In that moment, Kendra felt safe with Jamal. While he talked about his father, Kendra found herself suddenly falling in love with the man she'd once hid her heart from. And while Jamal was still talking about how difficult it was to grow up without a father, Kendra stopped walking, forcing him to stop. When Jamal turned around, she walked up to him and began to gaze into his eyes. The moment was electrifying and Jamal knew it was the moment he'd waited for. The two began to lean in, and just like that, they shared their first kiss. Three months later, Kendra did something she'd swore to herself that she wouldn't do. She lost her virginity to Jamal. At this point in their relationship, everything about Jamal mesmerized Kendra, and Jamal was also smitten. That's why the moment Kendra discovered that she was three months pregnant with Jamal's baby, they'd both celebrated. "I'm going to be here for you and our baby," Jamal proclaimed through teary eyes and an almost faint smile. "I love you, Kendra." Six and a half months later, Kendra gave birth to her first child, and Jamal's fourth child. And just like the rest of the women, Kendra gave birth to a little boy, and they'd decided to name him Jamal Jr. since Jamal didn't have a son named after him yet. Sadly enough, when Junior was a little over a year old, Jamal decided to end his relationship with Kendra. He'd met someone else, and he was in love with the new woman. All the same, he claimed that Kendra had been giving their son all of her attention. "It's like you forgot I existed," he'd said to Kendra after the two had broken up.

What happened here? I call this the Gradient of a Man's Heart. And by man, I mean male or female. Jamal was a great friend; in the friendship room, he was full of light (revelation) and love. And even though he shared intimate information with his friends, Jamal somehow managed to keep all of his friends in Circle 5. This is one of the reasons that most men have lifelong friendships with other males, but many (not all) of them have little to no emotional intelligence as it relates to women and Eros. Look at the Gradient of a Man's heart diagram (once again) to understand.

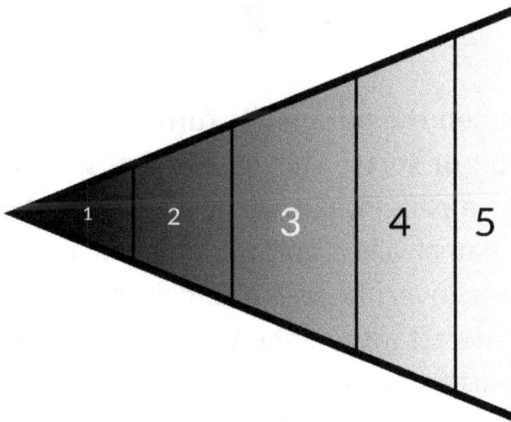

Notice that the closer you get to Level 1 of Jamal's heart, the darker it gets. This is because Jamal is a surface-level friend and lover. The only person who had been close to his heart had been his mother, and she'd traumatized him time and time again as a child. Remember, there are five levels to a man's heart, and let's say that Levels 1 and 2 are incredibly damaged because of relational trauma, but Levels 3, 4 and 5 have more light. Kendra was safe as Jamal's friend. Had she not crossed over into the intimate circle, she likely would have remained friends with Jamal for the rest of her life. But the minute she crossed the threshold of intimacy, she'd began to descend into the darkness.

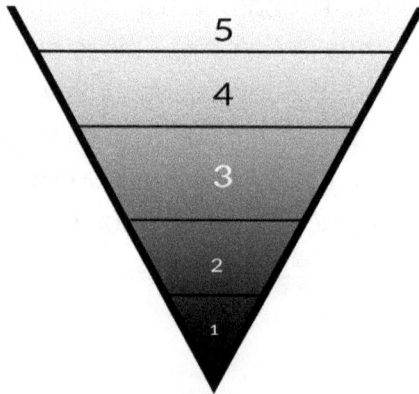

Notice that when the pyramid is turned vertically, it resembles a pit of sorts. This means that we are attracted to the light of a person, but we descend into the darkness. For example, Jamal was a great friend and an even better father, but as a lover, he was a complete monster. And if Kendra had paid attention, she would have discovered that Jamal had a pattern. His sons were 7, 4 and 2 years old. This means that there is a three-year distance between his first two sons, and a two-year difference between his middle child and his last son. What this says is that Jamal's relationships typically end when:

1. They reach the two or three-year mark.
2. When a child enters the picture.

In other words, in the beginning, Jamal is wholeheartedly sincere about his intentions whenever he meets a woman, but Jamal's core is rotten. So, whenever he dates a woman, he excitedly spoils her with gifts and beautiful words, but the closer that woman gets to his heart, the darker Jamal becomes. After a year or two, he almost becomes unrecognizable to his lovers. This means that while he has good intentions, Jamal's heart is a mess. This is because he has not allowed God to fill those dark spaces (voids). He's a surface-level Christian; he's allowed God into his intellect (this is why he memorized so many scriptures), but not into his heart. In other words, he has accepted Jesus as his Savior, but not his Lord.

The point is—you have to test the spirit of every person you meet, and don't give them access to roles and spaces in your heart that they do not qualify for. It doesn't matter how passionate they are about getting with you or how convincing they are when they claim to be changed men or women. Until you see the fruits of their choices consistently springing up, don't make any decisions regarding your relationship with them. Keep the guy in Circle 5 and solidify your boundaries any time he attempts to move closer. He has to prove himself to be mature enough, healthy enough and Godly enough to ascend from

Circle 5 to 4, and then to 3. Don't rush him through the circles, and don't allow him to rush himself through the circles. Your goal is to be patient and prayerful; this way, you won't ignore the condition of a person's heart, all the while forgetting to guard your own.

Relational Witchcraft

As I'm writing this, I am currently working on a seal order for a client of mine, and truth be told, I've thought heavily about refunding this particular client. By seal, I mean a logo for Bishops, Apostles and ministerial leaders. Why do I want to cancel her order? Simply put, she's a little too emotional for me, and this is always a red flag. The customer submitted a question via the contact form on my site, and I didn't respond to the message because I honestly forgot to. Nevertheless, she called my company's number the next day to ask her question, and while this is good, the first thing she did was use an inflected tone. She yelled, "I filled out the form yesterday because I need to get a Bishop's seal and a logo, and no one responded to me! I'm just looking for some help because I need to get this done pronto!" Mind you, I would have likely responded, after all, she'd submitted the form around 7:30pm the previous day and I found myself on the phone with her relatively early the next day. She paused for a second to hear what I would say, but I didn't say anything. I didn't feel like I had time to respond because she was talking so fast. All the same, just from her initial tone, I was sure of one thing—I didn't want to do business with her. "Hello?! Are you there?" she yelled. I sat up and adjusted myself in my seat. "Yes ma'am. I'm here." She paused again. I know that she was likely looking for an apology or some type of discount, and to be honest, apologizing would have been the right thing to do, but I recognized this behavior immediately. You see, I've been in business for well over 12 years, and anytime a person starts a call with extremely elevated emotions, that person is, in so many ways, demonstrating that he or she will not be easy to work with. You see, with these types of clients, they do want to order a logo, a website or whatever services you're offering, but what's more important to them is to dominate and control the people who work for them. They believe that the only way they'll get what they want is by inflating their tones and brandishing their emotions like blood-stained teeth. Could it have been a simple case of an upset client? Maybe, but again, emotional people are not easy to work with; they typically require, at minimum, four times the amount of time than most people. Nevertheless, I'm an entrepreneur, running a professional and ethical business, so I have to remain cordial, even when the client is behaving irrationally. She went on to tell me what she wanted, and anytime I tried to explain our prices and our policies, she would cut me off to say, "Yes, I know that already!" This is another red flag. In the world of business, one of the most beneficial lessons can be summed up with this familiar phrase, "All money ain't good money!" She required four times the amount of time over the phone as any other customer because she felt the need to control the conversation, nevertheless, I had to make sure that she understood our policies. You see, controlling people try to avoid the rules at all costs because they don't want (or plan) to abide by them. We finally got through the phone conversation, and later that day, I saw her order come in. I let out a dismal sigh as I clicked the form to see what she'd ordered. Her order was long and confusing. Not only had she not followed the rules, she requested two designs, not designating what elements were for one design versus what elements were to go on the second, plus, she'd only paid for one design. That was it! I told myself that I was going to just go ahead and refund her because we were off to a rocky start and I didn't want to spend the next few days of my life dealing with a lot of emotionalism, especially since I was trying to finish some other projects. I made up my mind to email her, explaining to her that my company was probably not going to be a good fit for her, and then I'd suggest a few other seal and logo designers for her to consider. But I decided to wait until later that evening; this way, I wouldn't end up having a draining conversation with her in the heart of the day. Later that evening, I decided to push past my frustrations and all the red flags and go ahead and attempt to create the design she'd ordered. But it was far too confusing, so I emailed her.

Why do I share this story? It's simple. By "her," I may be referring to a single woman, but I've worked with "her" many times. Not the person, but that particular spirit. I've had twelve years of experience dealing with emotional witchcraft, so whenever I come across a client who starts their orders off the wrong way, I do what Luke 14:28 says. "For which of you, intending to build a tower, sitteth not down first, and counteth the cost, whether he have sufficient to finish it?" This is emotional acuity. The following article was taken from Psychology Today:

> "Emotional intelligence refers to the ability to identify and manage one's own emotions, as well as the emotions of others. Emotional intelligence is

generally said to include a few skills: namely emotional awareness, or the ability to identify and name one's own emotions; the ability to harness those emotions and apply them to tasks like thinking and problem solving; and the ability to manage emotions, which includes both regulating one's own emotions when necessary and helping others to do the same" (Source: Psychology Today/Emotional Intelligence).

Emotional intelligence isn't just about navigating through conflict; the main objective of emotional acuity is discernment; this is so that you can avoid the wiles of the enemy, including emotional and relational witchcraft. In other words, the goal is to ensure that you don't find yourself entangled in an ungodly soul tie with another person, and to do this, you have to pay close attention to how a person talks to you, talks about others and how that person deals with conflict.

What are some of the symptoms and signs of relational witchcraft?

1. **Refusing to Answer Calls:** This includes not answering your phone calls, greeting you, responding to you, engaging with you on social media, etc.

2. **Behavior Shifts:** Let's face it. The people around us typically have habits that we've acclimated to subconsciously. But when someone wants to put another person on "punishment" or send a message to that person that he or she is upset, that

individual will suddenly stop doing what he or she normally does. For example, a man may be romantically pursuing a woman, but he hasn't fully made his interest known. Instead, he repeatedly flirts with her and sends her "good morning" texts. One day, he sees her at the office and notices a bouquet of roses on her desk. In this, he automatically assumes that the roses are from another man, so he suddenly stops sending the text messages. He reappears weeks later, saying something to the effect of, "Good morning. I hope I don't upset your boyfriend." In this, he has not only punished her, but he is indirectly questioning her about the roses. During the texting thread, let's say that the woman communicates that she doesn't have a boyfriend, and after he questions her about the flowers, she responds, "The flowers were from my team because my great aunt passed away." Not wanting to take accountability or appear to be emotionally immature, he will likely respond with, "I'm sorry to hear that. I honestly didn't know. I thought the flowers were from your boyfriend. I've been going through some changes myself. One of my cousins got arrested for theft, and it just seems like my whole family is going crazy." In this, he is attempting to explain away his sudden behavioral shift.

3. **Withdrawing One's Presence:** We see this behavior in our personal and professional relationships, whereas people will attempt to punish us by not showing up, for example, for church, for

an event, etc. This behavior is typically followed by a short or relatively long absence, whereas the person stops answering his or her phone calls, calling or showing up. If you don't pursue them, they typically reemerge after a few days to a few months, and when they do, they are oftentimes offended, and will say something to the effect of, "Why didn't you call to check on me?"

4. **Avoiding Accountability by Highlighting a Chaotic or Traumatic Event:** A good example of this behavior is when a woman cheats on her husband and disappears for a few days. She resurfaces several days later, and to avoid having a hard conversation, she may point out that someone close to her is sick or just passed away. The goal is not just to avoid accountability, but to transfer the guilt of her actions onto her husband, whereas, he is seen as insensitive if he dares to question her while she's worried, scared or grieving.

5. **The Infamous Cold Shoulder:** As one of the most common, normalized and accepted emotional witchcraft practices today, this tactic involves an individual making a communal space like a home, a business or any place where they gather with others uncomfortable by refusing to speak to their offender, refusing to communicate their offenses, slamming doors, etc. Please note that, as humans, we have habitats, and habitats are created by our habits. We naturally and instinctively set our environments to a certain temperature, spiritually speaking. For most of us, we thrive in peace, but

when someone engages in emotional witchcraft, that person will change the temperature in those communal spaces, thus making it difficult to occupy those spaces peacefully.

6. **Rejection**: People weaponize rejection or the fear of rejection to get what they want. For example, a man may start saying to his wife or girlfriend, "I've been thinking a lot lately, and I don't know if I can do this anymore. I think we may have to go our separate ways; at least, for a little while until I figure things out."

7. **Inflected Tones (Screaming)**: People tend to raise their voices in an attempt to get what they want, how they want it and when they want it.

8. **Name-Calling**: This particular method of emotional control typically precedes physical abuse. The objective behind name-calling is to deal a near-fatal blow to an individual's self-esteem through the use of words. This is typically done when the abuser inwardly fears the potential of the person he or she is abusing.

9. **Physical Abuse**: This is physically assaulting another person in an attempt to tame the person or teach the person a lesson. It is one of the highest or most notable mechanisms of control, and in so many ways, it is the abuser's attempt to physically incapacitate another human being or, in not so many words, communicate to that person that his or her life is in the abuser's hands.

10. **Withholding Sex**: Whenever one spouse decides to decline the sexual advances of another spouse

(except in cases when the other spouse is responding to adultery or abuse, or the couple has agreed to abstain so they can fast), that spouse is engaging in emotional witchcraft. Believe it or not, this is common. What does the Bible say about this? 1 Corinthians 7:3-5 reads, "The husband should give to his wife her conjugal rights, and likewise the wife to her husband. For the wife does not have authority over her own body, but the husband does. Likewise the husband does not have authority over his own body, but the wife does. Do not deprive one another, except perhaps by agreement for a limited time, that you may devote yourselves to prayer; but then come together again, so that Satan may not tempt you because of your lack of self-control."

11. **Behaving in a Nonchalant Manner**: In other words, when a person refuses to communicate with another person that he or she is intimately or intellectually connected with, but instead, shrugs and pretends that he or she no longer cares about the thoughts, welfare and actions of the other person or the state of their marriage, friendship, company, etc.

12. **Financial Abuse**: This is typically done when one spouse earns or controls all or most of the money that comes into a household. The abuser may begin withholding funds from the other spouse in an attempt to tame, train or punish that spouse. Another example of financial abuse is when one spouse purchases something like a house or a car, knowing that the other spouse could not afford to pay the notes or mortgage without him or her. Of

course, this is only witchcraft if that spouse is purchasing those things for that very reason; it is designed to keep the spouse financially tied to the other spouse.

13. **Reneging**: When one person suddenly changes his or her mind in an attempt to punish another person for offending him or her. (Example: After learning that his son wanted to remain in the custody of his ex-wife, James called his son to say that he wouldn't be able to attend his first football game).

14. **Abandonment**: In this, the abuser physically removes himself or herself from the victim for an extensive period of time. I refer to this technique as "tugging on the soul tie." The abuser's goal is to see how much control he or she has over the other person by withdrawing himself or herself from that person. Rarely does the person intend to be gone forever, but abusers will leave for extended amounts of time to teach their victims a lesson.

15. **Emotional Abandonment**: In most relationships, we have disagreements or, better yet, strife. A toxic or immature person tends to weaponize their lovers, friends or family members' emotions against them by creating high stress moments, and then emotionally abandoning those people in those moments. In short, what they do is they may go to sleep when you're extremely upset, turn on a comedy and laugh while you're in another room crying or get on the telephone and speak in a joyful tone with someone else after having spoken to you in a reproachful way.

16. **Destruction of Property:** Toxic people or abusive people will typically destroy any property that they feel their victims are fond of or anything they feel may serve to empower the people they are preying on. All the same, this method of abuse is designed to make their victims feel powerless.

17. **Idealizing an Ex:** This is one of the tools you'll typically find in a narcissist's bag of wiles. How this looks is—the narcissist will initiate a conversation about exes by first questioning their lovers regarding one or more of their exes. He or she may say, for example, "Tell me again why you and Sam broke up?" The narcissist is not interested in knowing or learning about the ex; he or she just wants to make the other person feel like they (the narcissists) have better options awaiting them. After their lovers have responded to them, talking about their exes, the narcissist will set the bait and wait for their lovers to ask them about one or more of their exes. If their lovers don't ask them, they'll interrupt them with something like, "Yeah, that reminds me of my ex—Toni. I thought we were going to be together forever because Toni and I just made sense. We never argued; she respected and supported my dreams, and I gave her my full support and respect regarding her dreams as well. She used to always laugh whenever I talked about scaling back on my dreams to build a family with her. She'd say, 'Boy, you know you'd be miserable stuck in the house! Nope, we can build a family, but there's no way I'm going to lock you in the house!

Nope! I'd push you to get out, chase your dreams and all, and I'll be home when you're ready to come home!'" In this, he would paint Toni as the perfect girlfriend, and whenever you questioned why they broke up, he'd likely say distance or he'd say, "I messed up." In this, the narcissist is simply saying that his or her soulmate is out there, so if things don't work between you and him, he has someone who's better suited for him than you at his beck and call.

18. **The Use of Tears:** Don't get me wrong; we all cry! We have to shed tears to grieve old mindsets, beliefs, relationships and realities. However, a person practicing emotional witchcraft will normally cry when they don't get their way or they may cry in public in an attempt to humiliate their lovers, family members, friends or complete strangers. One way to know that the person is engaging in emotional witchcraft is when the person is guilty of committing the offense, and then casts himself or herself as the victim, or this is a pattern of behavior that the person engages in.

19. **Fear Mongering:** My grandmother made the mistake of leaving my grandfather for a friend of his when they were older. At this time, my grandfather was experiencing the beginning stages of Alzheimer's disease. The man she left my grandfather for turned out to be incredibly insecure and abusive. One of his fear tactics was convincing my grandmother that the house they shared was haunted; he told her that certain areas of the house

or property were incredibly haunted. He reasoned that there was gold on the land and that the ghosts of the people who'd buried that gold there were guarding the gold. It wasn't until years later when I was an adult and my grandmother was no longer on this side of eternity that I realized that the man had likely hidden a lot of stuff around that house, and he used fear to keep my grandmother from finding it. He also forced her to wear his clothes, and she was not able to do much of anything with her hair or he'd accuse her of trying to impress another man.

20. **Seduction:** Promising sexual favors or being sexually suggestive in an attempt to extract something or a certain benefit from another person.

21. **The Use of "Flying Monkeys":** The following information was taken from PsychCentral: "Art imitates life and so it is with Flying Monkeys. The term was coined from the movie The Wizard of Oz in which the Wicked Witch dispatches monkeys to fly and get Dorothy and her dog. The monkeys obey her command, doing her dirty work for her, taunting and terrorizing Dorothy as she tries in vain to get back home. And so it is with narcissists and their flying monkeys. As if a magical spell has taken over, the bond between the narcissist and their flying monkeys is one of unwavering loyalty even in the face of danger. When the narcissist wants to evoke some punishment on a target they dispatch their henchmen (aka flying monkeys) to do their bidding. Unfortunately, this can and often does include abusive behavior such as guilt-tripping, twisting the

truth, gaslighting, assaults, threats, and violence. This keeps them out of harm's way and able to claim innocence if caught" (Source: PsychCentral/Narcissists and Their Flying Monkeys/Christine Hammond). In short, this is a method that's common to narcissists and toxic people, whereas they manipulate some of the people in their circles to exact punishment on another person who has offended them. This punishment can be something as light as having people to call and attempt to counsel the other person to sending someone to threaten and potentially harm the other person.

22. **Future Faking**: This is normally found in romantic relationships, and it takes place when one partner love-bombs the other partner with promises of them having a future together, and all that would come with it (houses, children, pets, etc.).

23. **Negative Body Language**: This includes frowning or unpleasant facial expressions or showing disdain, disinterest or disapproval for a person's words or choices through negative body language (crossing arms, avoiding eye contact, showing disinterest by focusing on something else, invasion of personal space, etc.).

24. **Withholding Children**: In this, one parent keeps another parent away from his or her own children in an attempt to control or punish the other parent.

25. **Over-Talking or Talking Too Fast**: How many times have you tried to engage in a conversation with a person, only to have that person repeatedly

cut you off with these words, "I'm sorry. I don't mean to cut you off," and then, they proceed to cut you off and express their own opinions? This would be fine if it happened once; it would even be understandable if it happened twice, but at some point during the conversation, you realize that the discussion is not only one-sided, but the person is completely disregarding or devaluing everything you say, and replacing it with their own beliefs. So, at some point, you decide to take your control back and keep talking, even when the individual in question attempts to interrupt you, but you immediately notice that the person is now huffing and being overly animated. That's a form of relational witchcraft. Anytime you come across the spirit of control, you will also find the spirit of witchcraft.

Believe it or not, this is just a short list of relational witchcraft practices, many of which have been normalized in our families and in our society as a whole. Relational witchcraft is centered around controlling others. Keep in mind that even God Himself does not control us. He gave us commandments and instructions to live by, but He also gave us a function called "will." With this particular function, we can choose to obey Him or choose to disobey Him. However, as the Word tells us, we will reap what we sow. In other words, there are sequences and consequences for every action. By sequences, I mean a particular order or action that follows another action. Another way to say this is, everything on Earth is a part of a system, and whenever a function is carried out, be it good or bad, it triggers another action or function, and this function triggers something else. This is what we call the domino effect.

In short, remember that every person in your life will show you, through their words and their actions, just how close to your heart they should be. If someone's presence in your life brings you a lot of pain, frustration or confusion, you need to push that person away from your heart. Remember, you would push them from, for example, Circle 1 to Circle 2 to see how they do there. If they are too immature for these particular circles, push them to Circle 3. Keep doing this until you find a space for them, even if that space is out of your life. If a person cannot handle Circle 5, it means that the person has no business being a part of your life, outside of being a demonic tool. It's okay to walk away from friends and loved ones when life calls for it. Some of the most productive and successful people will tell you that they've had to make some great and grand sacrifices to get where they are. It wasn't easy, but it was necessary!

SMALL-MINDEDNESS

Not everyone who behaves poorly is a wicked person. Some people are just small-minded. Earlier on, we talked about the different states of the human heart, which include, but are not limited to the parental state, the financial state, the mental state, etc. Each state has what can best be described as cities; these cities are what I call regions of thought. Every region of thought is either well illuminated, dim or dark. Remember that light represents revelation; it is the product of God's presence brought on through study and application. A dim city is the product of either:

1. Low-level revelation.
2. Double-mindedness.
3. Light from one of the neighboring regions of thought.

Each state is illuminated when we produce energy in that state, and I'm not talking about the New Age's depiction of energy. I'm talking about works, after all, James 2:26 tells us that faith without works is dead. Another way to say this is faith without works is dark. In other words, God is not present. This is why Romans 14:23 concludes with, "... for whatsoever is not of faith is sin." Hebrews 11:6 (ESV) states, "And without faith it is impossible to please him, for whoever would draw near to God must believe that he exists and that he rewards those who seek him." Imagine how Jesus would walk through what is now modern-day Israel, Palestine, Egypt and Lebanon. He is the Living Word of God, and in John 8:12, He says the following, "Then spake Jesus again unto them, saying, I am the light of the world: he that followeth me shall not walk in darkness, but shall have the light of life." Just as He navigated from city to city in the natural, we must allow Him to progress in our hearts spiritually. Whenever the Light of the World has not touched a city, there will be darkness. Again, another word for "darkness" is "void." And wherever there are voids, you will likely find a host of unclean spirits living in those voids or, at minimum, trying to enter into them. A lack of revelation, or better yet, a lack of God in an area creates a foul smell in that area that can be likened to the smell of death (decomposition), and this smell attracts devils. This is what Jeremiah meant in Jeremiah 17:9 when he said, "The heart is deceitful above all things, and desperately wicked: who can know it?" Consider Genesis 1. God created the Heavens and the Earth, and the Earth was without form and void, and darkness was upon the face of the deep. This is a clear depiction of what the heart looks like when it is dark. Imagine the mind as a map. Now imagine a bunch of states, all of which are divided into cities. Imagine that only a few of those cities are colored in or illuminated, indicating that there is life in those cities. This is what it looks like to be small-minded. Again, small-minded people aren't all bad; they simply don't know how to behave in some instances, and if they are demonically bound, what then happens whenever they come across a person who stands outside of their understanding, they will oftentimes draw from their limitations or their ignorance. And again, the word "ignorance" doesn't mean that a person is stupid; it simply means that information is present, but the person in question has chosen to ignore that information. For example, I grew up in Mississippi, which was and still is the poorest state in the United States. It is also the most racist state in the United States, which means that a lot of the Black population is still oppressed. One form of oppression is when a person or a group of people are intentionally restricted to a diet of revelation and/or information. Encyclopedia.com reports the following:

> "Anti-literacy laws varied from state to state. Virginia slave codes, for instance, required that 'any slave or free person of color found at any school for teaching, reading or writing by day or night' could be whipped, at the discretion of a judge, 'no more than twenty lashes' (Davis 1845, p. 3). Any white person found teaching 'free colored persons or slaves' to read could be fined between $10 and $100 and serve up to two months in jail. Mississippi state law required a white person to serve up to a year in prison as 'penalty for teaching a slave to read' (Davis 1845, p. 2). South Carolina law made it illegal for 'any assembly of slaves or freed persons of color to meet in secret or a confined space for mental instruction' (Davis 1845, p. 3)" (Source: Encyclopedia.com/Literacy and Anti-literacy Laws).

The following information was taken from the Oakland Literacy Coalition:

> "Confederate states in the antebellum South that passed anti-literacy laws included South Carolina, North Carolina, Georgia, Louisiana, Mississippi, Virginia, and Alabama. Due to fear following the

Stono Rebellion, the largest slave uprising in South Carolina in 1739, blacks were prohibited from learning to read. Plantation owners feared that literate slaves could write and use forged documents to gain their freedom. However, many of the enslaved used this method to obtain their freedom. Slave owner Hugh Auld describes this fear in this exchange with his wife, Sophia Auld, after he discovered her teaching a young Frederick Douglass how to read:

> He should know nothing but the will of his master and learn to obey it. As to himself, learning will do him no good, but a great deal of harm, making him disconsolate and unhappy. If you teach him how to read, he'll want to know how to write, and this accomplished, he'll be running away with himself. (Douglass, 2017, p. 14)."

Knowledge acquired by a slave was like a death knell to a slave owner. In order to destroy any semblance of humanity, plantation owners kept enslaved black people in the dark. The majority of enslaved people didn't even know the year they were born or their lineage. It was a purposeful removal of identity in an effort to perpetuate the slave mentality. Several confederate states jointly imposed literacy restrictions on the enslaved using legislation that went beyond the shackling of bodies and extended into the shackling of minds. In their attempts to shackle our intellect, they failed to factor in the resilience of a people who endured centuries of brutal dehumanization and forced assimilation. A paradigm shift occurs in the thinking processes of enslaved people who gain knowledge. Their thinking moves from a slave mentality to a mentality of liberation, thus making them "unfit to be slaves," as Frederick Douglass stated. (Source: Oakland Literacy Coalition/Literacy By Any Means Necessary: The History of Anti-Literacy Laws in the U.S).

Of course, this was slave-owners and former slave-owners attempt to maintain or regain control of Black people. This reinforced the beliefs that Blacks were animalistic and inferior to their White counterparts. And while anti-literacy laws no longer exist, the systems of anti-literacy are alive and well today. Keep in mind that Mississippi's public schools were not desegregated until 1970, and before desegregation, Black schools were given outdated books from White schools. Believe it or not, this was still taking place after I'd graduated high school. I'm not sure what year this (allegedly) took place, but I am confident that it was in the early 2000's when my former school, which was predominantly Black, ended up filing a lawsuit against the district because they discovered that the predominantly White school in our district was being supplied with new books, all the while, their old books would be transferred to my former school. To many of us, this was no surprise. Why am I sharing this? It is to say that small-mindedness is rarely, if ever, the product of one man being intellectually inferior to another man, it is simply the absence of information, whether that absence is intentional or simply just learned behavior. And I know that some people would argue this way, "Blacks have had a long time to educate themselves! Being ignorant is no longer an excuse!" To this, I say consider the following:

1. Blacks were and are still oppressed in many areas and industries.

2. We were raised by traumatized parents who had been raised by traumatized parents who had been raised by.... (you get the drift). In other words, just like many Whites are dealing with generational demons, the same is true for many Blacks.

3. Our ancestors had been enslaved by small-minded Whites. Notice that the Blacks whose ancestors migrated to the North in the 1800's and early 1900's fared far better than the ones who remained in the South. That's because open-minded Whites were typically open-minded because they were more educated. Therefore, a slave could not rise (in intelligence) above his or her master unless that slave had tutors or found some way to educate himself or herself.

4. One word ... capacity. When a person is raised by someone who has never tapped into their potential, that person will not know how to tap into his or her potential either. And the moment we all try to conquer regions of thought that have not been illuminated and inhabited (by God) for decades (centuries even), there is a great deal of warfare that the individual must face, not to mention the infamous learning curve. If a man or woman has never seen his or her parents overcome their demons, and that individual has never seen any

person who looks like him or her overcome their demons, chances are, that individual won't know how to overcome his or her own issues either. Nevertheless, we see a lot of people, both Black and White, overcoming their generational curses, strongholds and demons every day!

This isn't to point the fingers of blame or to bring up the subject of racism in America. It is to help us to understand what oppression looks like, after all, small-mindedness is oftentimes the result of oppression.

We all have a certain mental capacity. Think about our natural stomachs. How do they grow? They increase in size when we overeat. This is so the stomach can accommodate the excess food. This also causes the stomach to push against other organs in our bodies, thus making us sluggish and uncomfortable. What if I told you that the mind is similar to the stomach? As a matter of fact, your mind has its own digestive system. It takes in information, vomiting out anything you consider to be unpleasant, untrue or too controversial. Your appetite is determined by what you have stored in your heart. So, people with very little information or wrong information typically have small minds. This isn't to say that they are stupid, but it is to say that many people are ignorant. Again, the word "ignorant" comes from the root word "ignore," and it simply means that information is present, but a person has chosen to ignore that information. For example, racism is a form of ignorance. In it, the racist individual has decided not to educate himself or herself about other races, but has instead decided to perpetuate negative stereotypes about other races. This is an example of ignorance because there's tons of information available, but the person in question has chosen to disregard that information in favor of recycling what they've been taught or what they've told themselves.

Going back to the concept of states and regions of thought, whenever a city (region of thought) is dark, it will (more than likely) be inhabited by demonic forces. What this means is that whenever an individual attempts to illuminate that state by studying the Word of God, going to church, reading books, watching videos and getting mentorship, typically what happens is the person will experience the following:

- **The Stretching of the Mind**: This scary and uncomfortable experience is oftentimes enough to make a person stop trying. You see, the mind, like the stomach, has to be stretched, and whenever it is stretched, we typically feel the pressure of it stretching. This pressure includes loss of focus or inability to concentrate; it also involves fear, indescribable frustration, etc. This is the learning curve that we briefly spoke about.
- **The Voices in Our Heads**: Of course, these are the voices of demonic spirits mixed with our own voices that typically say:
  "You're not smart enough."
  "Why are you even trying?"
  "You will fail!"
  "This is too hard!"

"You look stupid!"

"At this point, you're just wasting your time and everyone else's time!"

"You're about to lose everything!"

"Why would God want to use you of all people?!"

- **The Crabs in the Bucket**: Slavery is a system, and I'm not just talking about the enslavement of Africans, I'm talking about the system of control. This means that even when people are released from physical bondage, they are almost always still in mental bondage to a set of beliefs, customs, traditions, theories and the like. Whenever someone tries to escape that bucket or limitation by studying information that is commonly not found in that region of thought, the people closest to that person will oftentimes ridicule, mock, sabotage and maybe even physically assault that person. A great example of this took place in slavery when some of the house slaves would snitch on the field slaves whenever they attempted to learn to read, escape or if they broke any of the rules.

- **Demonic Activity**: If all else fails, Satan's henchmen will oftentimes overwhelm a person by launching a series of attacks to keep that person from migrating from one mindset to another. Of course, the first series of attacks were mental, and then Satan used the familiar voices of those in our intimate circles, but when that didn't work, we started experiencing external warfare. This often looks like a financial attack or an attack against our character.

Small-minded people regurgitate and recycle the same experiences, the same information and the same relationships because they fear change. Many of them are incredibly intelligent, amazingly anointed and remarkably talented, but they have not learned to endure the pressures that come with starting over. Because of this, they lock themselves into seasons, thus causing those seasons to become strongholds. They hold tightly onto their relationships, even when many of them prove to be expired and toxic, and they typically justify their immobility with these words, "I love hard." A perfect example of a once small-minded person is Jonah. Let's look at his story.

- **Jonah 1:1-17:** Now the word of the LORD came unto Jonah the son of Amittai, saying, Arise, go to Nineveh, that great city, and cry against it; for their wickedness is come up before me. But Jonah rose up to flee unto Tarshish from the presence of the LORD, and went down to Joppa; and he found a ship going to Tarshish: so he paid the fare thereof, and went down into it, to go with them unto Tarshish from the presence of the LORD. But the LORD sent out a great wind into the sea, and there was a mighty tempest in the sea, so that the ship was like to be broken. Then the mariners were afraid, and cried every man unto his god, and cast forth the wares that were in the ship into the sea, to lighten it of them. But Jonah was gone down into the sides of the ship; and he lay, and was fast asleep. So the shipmaster came to him, and said unto him, What meanest thou, O sleeper? arise, call

upon thy God, if so be that God will think upon us,
that we perish not. And they said every one to his
fellow, Come, and let us cast lots, that we may know
for whose cause this evil is upon us. So they cast
lots, and the lot fell upon Jonah. Then said they unto
him, Tell us, we pray thee, for whose cause this
evil is upon us; What is thine occupation? and
whence comest thou? what is thy country? and of
what people art thou? And he said unto them,
I am an Hebrew; and I fear the LORD, the God of
heaven, which hath made the sea and the dry land.
Then were the men exceedingly afraid, and said
unto him, Why hast thou done this? For the men
knew that he fled from the presence of the LORD,
because he had told them. Then said they unto him,
What shall we do unto thee, that the sea may be
calm unto us? For the sea wrought, and was
tempestuous. And he said unto them, Take me up,
and cast me forth into the sea; so shall the sea be
calm unto you: for I know that for my sake this
great tempest is upon you. Nevertheless the men
rowed hard to bring it to the land; but they could
not: for the sea wrought, and was tempestuous
against them. Wherefore they cried unto the LORD,
and said, We beseech thee, O LORD, we beseech
thee, let us not perish for this man's life, and lay
not upon us innocent blood: for thou, O LORD, hast
done as it pleased thee. So they took up Jonah, and
cast him forth into the sea: and the sea ceased from
her raging. Then the men feared the LORD
exceedingly, and offered a sacrifice unto the LORD,

and made vows. Now the LORD had prepared a great fish to swallow up Jonah. And Jonah was in the belly of the fish three days and three nights.

Why did Jonah run from the voice of the Lord? We can only speculate at this point, but more than likely, he feared the faces of the people and he didn't want to leave his comfort zone. He didn't want to be Jonah, the prophet. He wanted to be an ordinary man living an ordinary life in his ordinary city. In other words, he was small-minded. You see, if you don't move around intellectually, you will become intellectually rigid or inflexible; this means that you will resist or vomit out any new information that threatens to alter your reality in any way. Understand that your reality is what's real to you. It is a combination of thoughts, beliefs and experiences that qualify you for the realm (state) you're in.

What are some signs and symptoms of small-mindedness? People who are small-minded:
1. Are easily offended or short-tempered.
2. Often serve as professional victims.
3. Have short attention spans.
4. Can be relatively argumentative.
5. Are oftentimes controlling.
6. Are oftentimes fearful.
7. Can be somewhat clique-minded (they hate making new friends).
8. Can wrestle a lot with entitlement.
9. Will often tolerate abuse simply because they don't want to start over or be alone.

10. Are terrified of a lot of things (birds, dogs, pools, etc.).

11. Have misplaced priorities; for example, a man with a small mind would be willing to spend $5,000 on car rims, but will not invest in his own education. He may be incredibly intelligent, but his priorities are misplaced.

12. Love money. What this means is that a small-minded person will steal, manipulate and kill to get his or her hands on money. And get this—there are small-minded millionaires out there, but the ones who are small-minded typically inherited, stole or married into their fortunes. Please note that the love of money is often rooted in trauma.

13. Love gossip. Busy people oftentimes don't have time for gossip, nor are they entertained by the misfortunes of others.

14. Are oftentimes the proverbial "crabs in a bucket."

15. Frequently uses profanity.

16. Are known to run away from problems quite easily.

17. Tend to wrestle with jealousy and comparison.

18. Typically live in the past, meaning they have trouble forgiving others.

19. Can be relatively vengeful.

20. Has difficulty taking accountability for his or her own wrongs, but instead points the fingers of blame at everyone else.

Again, this is just a short list. Why are we talking about small-mindedness? Because in order to be relationally intelligent, you have to learn how to test the capacity of another person's mind, especially if you are someone who doesn't plan to climax in life. And by climax, I mean that you don't plan to stop growing. Instead, you are trying to learn as much as you can, earn as much as you can and do as much as you can (in God's will, of course). If this is you, what you'll find is that you grow uncomfortable and maybe even be frustrated whenever you're engaging in certain conversations with small-minded people. I'm not saying that you don't like people; what I'm saying is you don't like small-talk and pointless conversations. You're not concerned with who's dating who or who cheated on who. You like forward-moving conversations that produce good results.

Small-minded people often use their emotions to control the people around them. They use inflected tones, threats of violence and a lot of emotional witchcraft to get their way. Why is this? Remember, whenever a person reaches the top of a season but refuses to graduate from that season, that person becomes a master of that season, or better yet, a master manipulator. In this, they become what Elijah would have become had he not left the Brook of Cherith once it dried up. He would have gone into survival mode. Consider how God led the Israelites out of Egypt. Exodus 14:19-20 reads, "And the angel of God, which went before the camp of Israel, removed and went behind them; and the pillar of the cloud went from before their face, and stood behind them: And it came between the camp of the Egyptians and the camp of Israel; and it was a cloud and darkness to them, but it gave light by night to these: so that the one came not near the other all the night." The light in the night represents revelation. When we follow closely up behind God, forsaking our own desires and fears, we are led by His revelation, but whenever we decide to turn a season into a comfort zone, revelation moves on. Consequently, we have to recycle the knowledge, understanding and information that we have and exchange it with people who are also stuck. When this happens one generation after the next, a generational curse is born, and along with that generational curse, man-made traditions, cultures and folklore are also born. And wherever and whenever you find the absence of revelation (light, God's presence), you will find an overabundance of the works of the flesh. What are the works of the flesh again? They are:

1. Adultery
2. Fornication
3. Uncleanness
4. Lasciviousness
5. Idolatry
6. Witchcraft
7. Hatred
8. Variance
9. Emulations
10. Wrath
11. Strife
12. Seditions
13. Heresies
14. Envyings
15. Murders
16. Drunkenness
17. Revelings

Another word for small-mindedness is little faith. Remember, the Bible talks about faith in varying sizes. Of course, faith without works is dead. Our minds stretch whenever we feed them with new information, especially if we continue learning and adding onto the information that we've stored. But a small mind sets the stage for a hard and prideful heart. The point is—if you want to maximize your time here on Earth, you have to allow yourself to be stretched repeatedly. You do this by studying the Word of God; this is what allows you to graduate from one realm or season to another. This is what Apostle Paul meant when he said, "Study to shew thyself approved unto God, a workman that needeth not to be ashamed, rightly dividing the word of truth" (2 Timothy 2:15). You must also gather what can be best described as secular knowledge (no, I'm not talking about demonic doctrines or lies). I'm talking about knowledge that doesn't fall under the category of being Christian. Depending on what mountain of influence or industry you're called to, you may have to learn things that make you uncomfortable so that you can be weaponized against the kingdom of darkness. This is what Apostle Paul meant when he wrote 1 Corinthians 9:19-23, which reads, "For though I be free from all men, yet have I made myself servant unto all, that I might gain the more. And unto the Jews I became as a Jew, that I might gain the Jews; to them that are under the law, as under the law, that I might gain them that are under the law; to them that are without law, as without law, (being not without law to God, but under the law to Christ,) that I might gain them that are without law. To the weak became I as weak, that I might gain the weak: I am made all things to all men, that I might by all means save some. And this I do for the gospel's sake, that I might be partaker thereof with you."

Never think that a person's mental capacity determines that person's value. Small-mindedness is honestly just a result of a person having limited experiences in life because of oppression (demonic or human), limited resources, a lack of education, trauma, delayed development and the list goes on. A small-minded person can grow in capacity if he or she is exposed to the right information and people. The process of growing one's mind can be somewhat uncomfortable, but over the course of time, people tend to adapt to change, so much so that they are no longer intimidated by the learning curves associated with growth, and they learn to welcome it with open arms.

And finally, don't try to fit big visions into small spaces. What I mean by that is, don't tell everyone what God has shared with you because not everyone can understand your vision. I think many of us have had to learn this the hard way. Love everyone, but learn to communicate with them according to where they are. This is why Apostle Peter told husbands to dwell with their wives "according to knowledge" (see 1 Peter 3:7). For example, I wouldn't share intimate details with a gossiper, nor would I get intimately involved with a professional victim. This means that I don't have to necessarily cut everyone off, I just have to place them in the right circles, and repeatedly remind myself of where they are emotionally and spiritually; this is so I don't get so carried away in a conversation with them that I divulge information that they are not mature enough to handle. For example, if I were to talk to an unsaved person, I wouldn't emphasize or even bring notice to the fact that I've been single for more than eight years because they'd try to "fix me up" with someone. And then, they'd fuss about my standards, so wisdom tells me to keep some things to myself.

Learn to recognize every person's capacity; this way, you don't put more responsibilities and expectations on them than they can bear. This is relational acuity. It allows us to preserve relationships with the people we love by learning to accept and respect where they are.

Relational Etiquette

I can remember sitting at the table with a millionaire for the first time. Well, this wasn't exactly the first time per se. In truth, I'd sat at some pretty significant tables, but this was the first time I'd been the centerpiece or the center of attention. This would be the first of two business meetings we'd have to discuss his book project. *How did I get here? Is this really happening?* I was besides myself with excitement, but I remained calm, answered all of his questions and tried to remember to keep my elbows off the table. In the end, I didn't get to work with him on his book project. During our second meeting, I found myself seated at a table in his office, surrounded by about five or more people. They asked me a ton of questions (rapid-fire) and I answered them all in detail. When the meeting was over, I rose from my seat and looked at all the smiling faces. They were all really nice; the meeting had gone well, but somehow I knew that I hadn't landed that particular contract. And truth be told, I wasn't all that disappointed because I was somewhat intimidated by the idea of working with someone of his stature (I was still a fairly new publisher). I knew he'd go with someone else when he'd asked me about my connections. He wanted someone with a large audience to promote his book, and my audience back then was about ten-thousand strong. During our first meeting, we had gone to a posh restaurant, and before we started talking about his book, we engaged in a little small talk while flipping through the menu the waitress had just placed in front of us. He was truly a nice man, and to my surprise, he was remarkably humble. I'd made up my mind that I was going to "foot the bill," but when I saw the prices, I almost choked on my soda. Nevertheless, I didn't show any signs of stress. For me, this would be a great investment. If nothing else, it would be a seed planted in fertile ground.

"Order whatever you want," he said. I knew that meant he planned to pay the tab, but my mind was made up. When that bill came out, my debit card was going to come out as well. Howbeit, I waited to see what he would order because I didn't want to order too much if he simply wanted to snack and talk, and I didn't want to order too little if he wanted to really dig in. After he ordered his food, I ordered what he'd ordered. At the table, we talked about his book, his expectations and what I could deliver. When the tab came, I saw him reaching for his wallet. "No, let me get it," I said, reaching into my purse to grab my debit card. He wouldn't hear it. He placed his debit card on the table and said, "Nope, I got it." On one hand, I wanted to gently pick up his card and hand it back to him, but I somehow knew better. I knew that I wouldn't impress him by insisting on paying the bill; I'd offend him instead. So, I thanked him as I pulled my wallet out to put my debit card back in it. A few years later, I would find my church home, and I'd listened as my pastor (Apostle Bryan Meadows) gave us a few lessons on relational intelligence. Listening to him, I realized that I'd passed the test a few years prior when I'd sat there with the millionaire, ready to prove myself worthy of being at that table. I also realized that I'd failed a few tests over the years. One of those tests had taken place in Germany, and I'd failed that particular test twice. I'd done so with pride, proving that I hadn't gotten out much over the course of my life.

The year was 2008 and I was in Ulm, Germany with the man I'd married a couple of months prior. I was just in town visiting for a couple of months when his landlord invited us over for dinner. The landlord's wife had cooked a huge dinner for us and everything looked immaculate. At this particular time in my life, I hadn't really visited too many places outside of Mississippi. Sure, I'd visited a few states outside of Mississippi, and I'd gone as far as Wisconsin twice, but other than that, I was pretty untraveled and uncultured. So, when the hostess placed a bowl of soup in front of me, she didn't realize that she was about to be in for a treat. After everyone had been served, we all grabbed our silverware and began to eat.

"You embarrassed me!" It was about an hour or so later, and Monty and I were on our way back to his place. I stopped and stared at him as he continued walking. "How did I embarrass you?!" I asked defensively. You see, people who haven't traveled much tend to be headstrong and prideful, and that I was! "I kept trying to get your attention," he countered. "You ate the soup with the dessert spoon! I was so embarrassed!" A normal person would have taken the critique and learned from it, but at that time, the only thing I could seem to hear was the word "embarrass." A year later, I would repeat this same crime while living in Eberbach, Germany with Monty. Again, we'd been invited somewhere to eat, but this time, at the home of Monty's manager. Unlike last time, Monty didn't wait to correct me. He leaned over and whispered in my ear, "You're embarrassing me again." You're eating the soup with the dessert spoon. I laid the spoon back down and grabbed the correct spoon. Was Monty a bad guy for correcting me? No. His approach the first time wasn't ideal, but it hadn't been over-the-top either.

I shared this story to show you what pride looks like. In this, I was so proud of where I'd come from that I thought I needed to represent what I didn't know, rather than learn something new. Pride causes people to be relationally retarded, meaning they try to prove their loyalty to the limited spaces they've come out of by serving as ambassadors whenever they enter into new spaces. By doing this, they dishonor the tables that they are invited to. Not realizing it, they exalt their own cultures and beliefs, all the while demeaning and diminishing the cultures and belief systems in the spaces they've been invited into. This was what I'd done—twice! Consequently, the next time we had been invited out again, we'd found ourselves in the house of one of his coworkers, and that experience was more than uncomfortable. This is because his coworker kept trying to get us drunk. Thankfully, I refused to drink, but my ex kept drinking, even though I'd pleaded with him to take it easier. And even when he was tipsy, the coworker felt like he needed more to drink. At the same time, the coworker and his girlfriend were a little too flirty for me. I could tell that they were into some pretty "weird stuff" because the boyfriend kept invading my personal space, giving me the most awkward eye contact and making remarks about me and Monty's sex life. And he couldn't seem to stop touching my hand! I could feel myself getting upset because every time Monty said that he didn't want anything else to drink, the guy would pour him another drink and insist that he drink it. He'd tried that with me as well, but I'd refused repeatedly. I didn't have a single drink, but Monty could barely stand because of all the drinks he'd had. The host looked at me and said in the most sensual tone, "You can spend the night if you want. We have space." We'd declined this offer many times, and every time we did, he would pour Monty another drink. Thankfully, Monty sobered up enough for us to make it to the bus stop so we could go home, but that experience was one of the most uncomfortable experiences I'd ever had.

Why did I share this story? In short, I'd dishonored the honorable and good tables I'd sat at by refusing to learn about the different types of silverware, and then becoming argumentative whenever I was corrected. While this may seem small and insignificant, dishonor is a major crime to commit against any person and/or organization. Not to sound like I'm reaching, but because I had not respected those spaces, I found myself in a seedy environment trying to sober up the man I was married to just to keep us from being taken advantage of.

This is what those experiences taught me:
1. Study the tables you're going to sit at before you're invited to them; this way, you can properly prepare

yourself for them. In other words, learn both basic and not-so-basic table manners.

2. Never exalt your culture over someone else's culture. It's not only rude, it signifies that you are relationally underdeveloped.

3. Heal so that you won't bleed on anyone's table. What this means is—your conversations are oftentimes a product of your experiences, and believe it or not, whenever you don't know what to say, you may end up drawing from your past and saying the wrong things.

4. It's okay to say no. It will protect you from having a few uncomfortable story times with your therapists, doctors or your closest friends.

5. Never try to exalt yourself at a table; if the main host insists on paying, let him or her do so.

6. Some tables are designed to give you a glimpse into where God intends to take you.

7. Don't let your introversion stifle you. Go into some crowded spaces and allow yourself to be surrounded by the very thing that makes you uncomfortable: people. For example, during my first meeting with the millionaire, he was sold on the idea of me publishing his book, but our second meeting was at his church and he'd invited quite a few people to aid him in making his decision. Again, while his decision to not work with me was primarily based on the fact that I only had ten-thousand followers and, according to him, one of his sons in the faith had far more followers and would be a better pick at promoting his book, I can honestly say that me

being surrounded by a bunch of people bombarding me with questions wasn't exactly a highlight moment of mine. Don't get me wrong, I'd done really well because I'd intentionally placed myself in some uncomfortable situations before, but I would have done far better had I been better prepared, after all, I thought we'd meet at his church and he'd interview me again by himself. I thought that the only other person who would be at the church would be maybe his secretary or a few janitors. I was completely taken aback when I walked into a room and saw no less than seven people sitting at a table inviting me to sit down.

8. Wait for the host or the person you're entertaining to order his or her food before you order yours.

9. Learn about table utensils and which ones you should be eating with at any given time.

10. Give eye contact and remain engaged while talking with the people at the table.

11. If you don't know the answer to a question, simply say, "I don't know, but I'll find out" or go to Google from your phone to conduct a quick search.

12. It is never a great idea to be nervous. Understand that fear will cause you to make a bunch of silly mistakes like spilling your drink, tripping over your left foot or saying something inappropriate.

13. Always offer to pick up the tab when the host outranks you or if you're trying to secure a business contract. Manipulating the host into picking up your tab will almost always serve as a red flag to the

host. Consequently, you may lose a big contract over a $50 meal.

14. Dress properly for where you're going.
15. Put your pride away; pride closes doors; it does not open them.

Healing Relational Wounds

One of the most important lessons you'll ever learn is this—expectation sets the stage for disappointment. Disappointment, when left untreated, can create a bunch of trauma wounds. Trauma wounds set the stage for trauma-bonds (soul ties with toxic people), and trauma bonding only leads to more trauma. It is the gift that keeps on giving!

As I mentioned earlier, my mother was an amazing woman, and I thank God for her life. What I honor and respect about her the most is how much she sacrificed to ensure that my siblings and I had a roof over our heads and food on our plates. She often worked two jobs to make ends meet. However, like many American families, our family was incredibly dysfunctional. I can remember watching my Mom come home from McRae's (her main job) on some days. She'd be carrying large bags as she made her way towards her bedroom. I'd excitedly sprint from my bedroom, thinking that she'd purchased something for me. Instead, I'd watch as she pulled out one outfit after the other for my little sister. My sister would dance with excitement as my mother held up the clothes she'd bought for her. Unbeknownst to me, I was the infamous "lost child" in the toxic family dynamic. Check out the following information about the roles in the toxic family:

"The Lost Child

The Lost Child is usually known as "the quiet one" or "the dreamer". The Lost Child is the invisible child. They try to escape the family situation by making themselves very small and quiet. (S)He stays out of the way of problems and spends a lot of time alone. The purpose of having a lost child in the family is similar to that of The Hero. Because The Lost Child is rarely in trouble, the family can say, "He's a good kid. Everything seems fine in his life, so things can't be too bad in the family."

This child avoids interactions with other family members and basically disappears. They become loners, or are very shy. The Lost Child seeks the privacy of his or her own company to be away from the family chaos. Because they don't interact, they never have a chance to develop important social and communication skills. The Lost Child often has poor communication skills, difficulties with intimacy and in forming relationships. They deny that they have any feelings and "don't bother getting upset." They deal with reality by withdrawing from it.

In an NPD family, The Lost Child just doesn't seem to matter to the narcissist, and avoids conflict by keeping a low profile. They are not perceived as a threat or a good source of supply, but they are usually victim of neglect and emotional abuse. (Source: Out of the Storm/Dysfunctional Family Roles).

Note: The aforementioned website details all of the roles in the toxic family unit, so be sure to check it out. I only listed the role that I mentioned (lost child) so that I could avoid infringing on their rights, given the fact that the article is pretty extensive.

"Mom, what did you buy me?" I'd ask, hoping that she'd maybe left some bags in the car. She'd look at all the items she'd dumped on her bed. "I bought us some stockings and socks," she'd say, pointing at all of the pantyhose and socks she'd purchased. She always bought home pantyhose and socks, after all, this was the department she worked in. All the same, being a household of women, we all shared the socks and stockings. I could feel the hurt and the disappointment in my chest. I'd whine and complain sometimes, but in most cases, I would simply just head back to my bedroom disappointed. As I mentioned earlier, when I was 15-years old, I had a shift in my mentality, and I think it was around that time when I stopped setting myself up for disappointment whenever I heard her coming into the house with bags. I reasoned with myself that if she had anything for me, she'd let me know. In truth, by doing this, I found myself feeling better emotionally and this prevented the arguments that would break out whenever I used to gleefully barge into her bedroom thinking she'd bought me an outfit or two. Over the course of time, this became a system in my life.

Now, don't feel sorry for me! I believe that I am the strong, God-fearing and responsible person I am today because I learned young that nobody owed me anything and that if I wanted something, I needed to get up and work for it. I had to get it for myself (with God's help, of course)! And that mindset shift has really helped me to not be easily offended or easily hurt by the choices of people. Eventually, I learned that my family had the classic toxic family makeup, which included the scapegoat, the forgotten or lost child and the golden child. When I first learned about this dynamic, I screamed in amazement. It was, at minimum, comforting to put language to what I'd experienced growing up. Howbeit, I know my mother wasn't trying to be malicious. When I was an adult, she explained it this way, "She (referencing my sister) needed me more than you did," she'd told me after we'd spoken about her showing favoritism towards my sister when we were younger. When I grew up and moved out, my mother and I talked about my childhood, and one day, she apologized. Thankfully, we had a pretty good relationship all the way up until her passing.

Can you imagine the relational wounds Isaac must've had after his father, Abraham, tried to sacrifice him? Of course, Abraham had not been wrong; he was simply obeying God, and thankfully, God intervened before Abraham could kill his son. Can you imagine the relational wounds that Joseph must've had after being assaulted by his brothers, tossed into a pit and then sold off into slavery by the men he'd grown to know as his siblings? How about the relational wounds that Esau experienced after his mother helped his brother to steal his birthright? This is to say that if you've come from a broken, toxic or dysfunctional family, you are in good company! Please note that you don't have to continue to tolerate dysfunction, however. As a matter of fact, I advise against it! You simply need to establish and solidify a set of boundaries and communicate them with the members of your family. The next part is the hardest; you have to repeatedly enforce those boundaries until your family realizes that you won't budge from them, so they'll either learn to respect those boundaries or they'll put distance between themselves and you. And while this does hurt, it works out for your betterment in the end because you'll soon discover (after you heal and make peace with your situation) that you function and thrive better in peace.

Now, let's talk about how to heal relationship wounds once and for all. Below are some of the approaches I took to start and complete my healing journey:

1. **Pray**. You need God every step of the way.
2. **Study the Word daily.** In the beginning, the Word was with God and the Word was God. Who is God? The Bible gives us many descriptions and names for Him, with one of those descriptions being Light. Now, He's not the sun and He's not the moon, even though He created them. He is the Source of all things (Abba). We were created in His image, so we can't function properly without Him. This is to say that it is His Word that illuminates the dark places in our hearts; it is His Word that casts out demons, and it is His Word that transforms us.
3. **Don't miss church or Bible study!** Some people argue that they can study from home, but the Bible tells us not to forsake the gathering of the saints

(see Hebrews 10:25) and to refrain from leaning to our own understanding (see Proverbs 3:5). Let's not forget that the Bible tells us in Proverbs 4:7, "Wisdom is the principal thing; therefore get wisdom: and with all thy getting get understanding." Lastly, Ephesians 4:11-15 states, "And he gave some, apostles; and some, prophets; and some, evangelists; and some, pastors and teachers; for the perfecting of the saints, for the work of the ministry, for the edifying of the body of Christ: Till we all come in the unity of the faith, and of the knowledge of the Son of God, unto a perfect man, unto the measure of the stature of the fullness of Christ: That we henceforth be no more children, tossed to and fro, and carried about with every wind of doctrine, by the sleight of men, and cunning craftiness, whereby they lie in wait to deceive; but speaking the truth in love, may grow up into him in all things, which is the head, even Christ." In other words, don't depend on yourself, don't isolate yourself; go fellowship with other believers and learn the Bible more intently.

4. **Forgive from the heart, and do it fast!**
   Forgiveness is not something we can do on our own; this is why we need the Holy Spirit. Ask the Lord to help you to forgive everyone who's hurt you.

5. **Close doors.** You can't heal in the environment or around the people who hurt you. It's okay to let people go. Yes, even if they're relatives (this includes parents).

6. **Move the rest of the people around in your life so you don't have to keep forgiving them**. The truth is—some people aren't bad. They just aren't mature enough to be that close to your heart. Reposition them to Circles 2, 3, 4, 5 or out of your life, if the occasion calls for it!

7. **Get a therapist**. Even sane people need therapy to remain sane! Therapy is all about rebuilding and sustaining a healthy mind.

8. **Create a personal constitution, detailing what you will and will not allow**. Write the vision; make it plain, and then execute it.

9. **Now, set the boundaries, solidify them and enforce them**. Without boundaries, you are what the Bible calls a city without walls. "He that hath no rule over his own spirit is like a city that is broken down, and without walls" (see Proverbs 25:28).

10. **Give them grace**. Most people deserve a chance to change, but this doesn't mean that they have to be granted this opportunity from up close. Point them to a therapist, invite them to church, talk with them about Jesus and encourage them with kind words. Get this—what you've done is just prepared a plate for them. Now, watch to see if they want what's on that plate and how much of it they eat! If they don't make any efforts to change their lives, be sure to change their roles, responsibilities and positions in your life.

11. **Learn as much as you can about what you've experienced**. For example, if you had narcissistic parents, purchase books and watch videos about

narcissism and the Jezebel spirit. Familiarize yourself with the language of that world, remembering that ignorance is the devil's favorite hiding place.

12. **Find and join communities (support groups) of like-minded people who can relate to what you've experienced and encourage you through it.** Warning: if you've come through narcissistic abuse, many support groups will be filled with broken and even narcissistic people. Be kind, but don't forget to keep everyone in Circle 5, and only bring the ones closer over time who prove themselves to be Godly and mature enough to occupy that space. No trauma bonding!

13. **Lower your expectations, but raise your standards.** People often do the exact opposite, whereas they raise their expectations, all the while lowering their standards, thus setting themselves up for repeated disappointments. For example, I stopped expecting my mother to buy clothes for me, so whenever she didn't buy me anything, I wouldn't feel hurt or disappointed, but on those rare occasions when she did buy me something, I was truly appreciative. Adjust your expectations to fit their habits, but raise your standards. If what they repeatedly give to the relationship does not meet your standards, reposition them in your life. Another example of this is—if your child's father is a repeated no-show whenever his day of visitation comes, stop expecting him to show up. All the same, raise your standards by requiring that he

communicate his intentions with you 48 hours in advance, and then record any and every absence.

14. **Count the costs before you build a thing; this includes relationships and allowing people to enter into a more intimate space in your heart.** This is a biblical principle (see Luke 14:28) that most believers truly do not understand or apply. Consequently, as believers, we spend more time recovering from trauma than we should.

15. **Get wise counsel.** I can't emphasize this enough. Ask the Lord to lead you to your wise counselors, and be sure to honor them, listen to their counsel and apply that wisdom. And by honoring them, I also mean, don't be a consumer in their lives. Don't consume their time and their resources without blessing them in return. Remember this principle— never say "thank you" more than you say "you're welcome."

16. **Do something different!** Sometimes, recycling the same experiences only brings back memories. Get out and do something you've never done before, go places you've never gone before and envision something you've never considered before. Lifestyle changes are amazing! Change your eating habits, get out more, learn a new language, visit other countries, learn a new skill, go back to school—just get out and live!

17. **Stop lying to yourself!** Toxic people don't get better over time(unless they willfully pursue Jesus). Stop holding onto your fantasy of a person, and take a second look at that person's reality. This will

force you to make a sober choice. For example, a woman with an abusive husband should stop fantasizing about him becoming a great husband, and ask herself this question—am I willing to be abused for the rest of my life or potentially killed? Can I accept this man as he is, or am I pining away for who I think he has the potential to become?

18. **Practice using your voice.** Understand that the word "no" is authoritative. It is so powerful that it causes the spirit of offense to rise up in people, and it causes many of the people who are not supposed to be in your life to walk away. It also causes those in your life to get in their rightful positions (Circle 1, 2, 3, 4 or 5).

19. **Volunteer somewhere; help others.** There is so much healing power in helping others, but when we're wounded, we can be considerably selfish. Pick yourself up and push yourself to volunteer at your church, a soup kitchen, a shelter or wherever you find people in need of assistance.

20. **Keep giving God your "yes."** While on this journey, I've experienced several storms, many of which brought me to the intersection of a decision. At this crossroads, I could hear God asking me if I wanted to continue or if I wanted to stop where I was. Even though I was feeling defeated, frustrated and overwhelmed, I have always given God my immediate "yes" because I know that He's with me every step of the way. In other words, don't give up, don't give in and don't become the very thing that hurt you.

And finally, one important question that you have to ask yourself is this—do I truly want to be healed? Why is this important? I've counseled my fair share of people over the years, and I was taken aback when I first realized that a lot of people do not want to heal; they simply want to talk about what happened to them and how they feel about it—repeatedly. I've given them the tools to move forward, including recommending them to therapists and other counselors, only to discover that they did not utilize those resources. So, I asked them an important question, "What do you really want?" What I discovered was that, without saying it, most of them wanted one or more of these four things:

1. To control the Most High God.
2. To control the people around them.
3. Lots and lots of attention.
4. Pity.

This meant that there was no viable way to satisfy them. They would have to be tormented until they decided to submit to God, instead of demanding that He submit to them. I've watched people isolate themselves in communal settings, and then whine and complain about no one checking on them. I soon learned the logic behind this mentality. I realized that a lot of people pitch tents in churches and programs, but they refuse to come out of those tents. Those tents represent mindsets and those tents typically have a two-person capacity. What this means is—they don't want to come outside of their comfort zones to heal. Instead, they want God's leaders to come and camp with them. The problem with this is, there would be no forward movement for anyone else if the leaders did this. Simply put, they want company, not help. I'm saying that to say this—make sure that you genuinely want to heal and move forward. If not, be sure to set up as many therapy sessions as possible so that you can come out of that dark space. The goal is to heal and grow so that you can be an example to others.

Breaking Relational Curses

"Just like that?" Zuri asked, searching the eyes of her husband. "After 17 years of marriage, three children and all that we've been through, you want to end it all just like that?" The hurt in Zuri's voice became increasingly evident with every word she spoke, and Angelo, her husband, didn't have an answer for the woman he now wanted to part ways with. Zuri waited another minute before speaking again. "Okay," she sighed. "There's nothing I can do or say. You've made up your mind. I guess now the only thing we can discuss is who gets what in the divorce." Those words pierced Angelo's soul. On one hand, he didn't want to divorce his wife, but on the other hand, he felt helpless, worthless and confused. He'd lost his job a year prior, and Zuri had been paying all of the household bills by herself. He'd taken on the role of being the homemaker, but he sucked at it, and because of this, Zuri would oftentimes come home and have to clean up the house to her liking. Plus, he'd never been that great at math, science or social studies, so again, Zuri had to step in to help the children. The only thing he felt that he was contributing to his wife was sex, and lately, it almost felt to him like he had been failing in that arena since Zuri was rarely in the mood. So, Angelo met a woman one day while taking his morning jog, and the two of them had hit it off pretty well. Now, four months later, he was sure of one thing—he wanted to be with his mistress, Carmen.

Before we go any further into this story, let's look at the men in Angelo's lineage. Angelo's father had been married to his mother for 13 years, and one day, he'd gone to work, but he never came home. Four years later, he filed for divorce after his wife found his current address three states away in New Mexico. He had been living there with his mistress, and the two of them had two children by the time his wife found him. His grandfather hadn't left his grandmother; instead, he'd abused and cheated on her so much that she'd committed suicide after nine years of marriage. She'd done this after learning that his mistress was at a hospital nearby giving birth to his son. His great-grandfather had been the ultimate womanizer. Even though he was once married to Angelo's great-grandmother, he'd managed to have ten outside children with ten different women! And then, there was Angelo's great-great grandfather, Lloyd. Mr. Lloyd had once served as a slave, and not just any slave, but a stud. This means that he had been used to breed with multiple women because he was considered strong and believed to have strong genes. So, as you can see, Angelo's paternal bloodline had been riddled with broken marriages and relationships, so it should have been no surprise to Zuri that her husband would follow in his father's footsteps, after all, these had been the steps that had been modeled for him.

But wait!!! Zuri would argue that Angelo promised that he would be different; he wouldn't be like his father! And he had been convinced of this, even pursuing Zuri with intensity when she'd tried to end their relationship after two months of dating because of her fear surrounding his lineage and his many failed relationships. Nevertheless, with tears in his eyes and 12 long stem roses in his hands, Angelo had managed to make his way to the other side of town, go to Zuri's job and plead for her to change her mind. And he'd done this in front of thirty blushing women who all wished they could trade places with Zuri at that time. Howbeit, here she was 17 years later, and all of her fears regarding their relationship were coming to life. "I ... I don't want a divorce," Angelo said sheepishly as he lowered his head to the floor. "I just need some time..." Angelo's words cut Zuri to the core. She turned to walk away from the man who would soon become her ex-husband, but just as she took her second step, she became overwhelmed with emotions. "Time?!" she shouted, turning back to look at her husband. By now, the whites of her eyes had turned red and the tears that she'd managed to so courageously hold back were streaming down her face. "Let me get this straight—you want me to sit around this house losing my mind while you're out there entertaining another woman?! You want me to wait for you to finish having fun with her so you can play eeny meeny miny moe with our hearts? Who do you think you are?! Angelo, I'll be okay! Just leave! I should have listened to my instincts 17 years ago! Did you hear me?! Just leave!" With those words, Zuri watched as Angelo slowly made his way towards the living room door. Just as he was about to walk out of the door, he looked back at his wife. "I do love you," he said, before disappearing into the dark night.

I would love to tell you that Angelo and Zuri's story has a happy ending. I know many people would love to hear how Angelo eventually reaped what he'd sown, and how Zuri had gone on to find love with a man who was more Godly and mature than the man who'd betrayed her. But that's not necessary, and here's why—Galatians 6:7 reads, "Be not deceived; God is not mocked: for whatsoever a man soweth, that shall he also reap." I have lived on the face of this Earth long enough to say that the law of sowing and reaping is absolute, meaning it is immutable. This is because it is a law. Therefore, whenever I'm counseling or encouraging people whose spouses have betrayed and abandoned them, I always lead with or leave them with these words, "Forgive. Heal. Keep moving forward, and let God do what He's going to do in that person's life. Just don't look back." In other words, I am absolutely convinced that the offender will have his or her day, but at the same time, I'm not relishing in the fact that the person will reap what he or she has sown. My sincerest wish is that the person I'm encouraging heals, and that the offender surrenders his or her life to Christ, after all, a surrendered heart is a repentant one. But this chapter isn't about Angelo getting what the old folks used to refer to as his "come-uppings." Instead, my goal is to point out a fact so potent that it can help you in your future relationships or your marriage. What fact is that, you ask? The nature of a generational curse (relationally speaking).

Everything we approach has a measure of light. For example, if you have been married for four years, the fifth year (at this moment) has the measure of light that your parents provided through their marriage. So, if your parents were married for 45 years and they never divorced, every year you're married will look bright to you because your parents have already paved the way and illuminated the path for you. If, on the other hand, your spouse's parents divorced after 11 years of marriage, you will likely notice a shift in your spouse's attitude as you approach the ninth and tenth year. This is because your spouse doesn't know what a lifetime commitment looks like. Think of it this way—imagine that every year that the two of you overcome the odds is a year that's illuminated for the children that you both share. This is because they get to watch you walk, skate, crawl and kick through the many obstacles that they will someday face. However, if your marriage ended, for example, at year six, the sixth year and any year after that will be incredibly dark and unpredictable. This then creates a gradient effect for your children, whereas whenever they get married, they will likely find that every year that they're married will appear to be darker, gloomier and scarier than the previous one.

How would you overcome this curse? It's simple. You would need to find someone to mentor you who's gone further than you and your spouse in marriage. For example, if your parents divorced when you were three-years old, chances are, you would become almost impossible to live with after year two. Now, in your mind, you'd be the perfect wife or husband, but your spouse would likely beg to differ. You could potentially become more demanding and more controlling, and this would all stem from fear. You see, whenever we can't see what's ahead of us, we are oftentimes arrested by fear, and this causes us to become all the more controlling. And what makes this even more detrimental is the fact that most of us tend to focus on our intentions, not our actions. This is why we often see ourselves as victims when our relationships fail. We think about the great fight that we put up to hold our marriages together and the many times we'd tried to turn a negative moment into a positive one, not realizing that we put so much pressure and so many rules on our spouses that they didn't know anything else to do but run. The same is true for the men and women that we will someday marry or are already married to. If you're a married woman, it is important for you to know how long your husband's parents were married; that is if they were married, of course. This information could help you to understand his behaviors as you both press through the years. If his parents were only married for eight years, you have to pay attention to the way he processes information and conflicts, especially around the five-year mark. This is because every year approaching the eighth year is darker than the previous year for him. At some point, he will have the responsibility of walking by faith, thus creating the light or revelation that your children will someday follow. But, get this—he would likely need a mentor to help him as he entered into nothingness. This mentor should be a man who's been married, for example, for 30 plus years. This mentor would then help to illuminate the path for him, thus removing the fears and insecurities that are lurking up ahead. Please note that a large number of men don't communicate their fears to their wives out of fear of being seen as less than men. This means that they erroneously try to fight those battles alone. If you are married, it is a great idea to help your husband feel safe whenever he communicates with you. You do this by not rehashing or weaponizing anything he's shared with you.

Remember that curses are spots in time or seasons that are dark; this means that God has removed Himself from a situation, a relationship, a person or an era because of sin or rebellion. To break relational curses, you simply have to:

1. Repent of your sins, the sins of your parents and the sins of your ancestors. Sure, you are not guilty of their wrong doings, however, the purpose of repenting on behalf of them is to address the sin at its root. The goal is to break the curse of iniquity.

2. Renounce your sins, the sins of your parents and the sins of your ancestors.

3. Submit yourself to God in the areas in which you sinned.

4. Resist the temptation of the enemy to return to the ditches that God has pulled you out of.

5. Get yourself a mentor and don't let go of that mentor unless the Lord tells you to!

6. Honor the mentors and leaders that God brings into your life. Never allow entitlement or offense to corrode your soul ties with them.

7. Study to show yourself approved for every season (mindset) that you want to enter. New mindsets equal new realities. New realities are the products of new realms. New realms present new opportunities. New opportunities set the stage for

new experiences. New experiences create sparks; these sparks are a culmination of joy, happiness and peace. When they form, they set us on fire for God.

8. Refuse to climax in any given season. Remember, if you master a season, it's time for you to become a student in another season. If you refuse to move, you will become a master manipulator in a season, and while you may be popular, you will become a villain or crab-in-a-bucket for everyone who attempts to go higher than you.

9. Remember that the greatest enemy of a child of God, especially one who's anointed to do remarkable things in the Earth, is comfort. Comfort zones are beautifully decorated prisons and graves where the anointed go to die. When their zeal dies, it releases a stench called entitlement, and entitlement ushers in the spirits of witchcraft and control.

10. Pray without ceasing. This means that you shouldn't put a schedule on prayer. Sure, it's okay (and even recommended) that you pray in the morning and in the evening before you go to bed, but these shouldn't be the only times that you pray. To pray without ceasing means that you need to be open and willing to pray throughout the day whenever you see or feel the need to intercede.

WHAT TO EXPECT ON THIS JOURNEY

To understand this chapter, you must understand how seasons work. Seasons are cycles of information that we consume and regurgitate. Seasons are all about information! Can you speed your way through a season by overloading yourself with new information? Not really. All of the information you take in has to be consumed and then processed and expressed. This is what alters the shape of your belief system. The alteration of your belief system is called transformation. What does this mean? The information must be digested. In other words, you must extract revelation from what you've learned. This is what brings that information out of the waiting room of the soul (conscious) into the heart or, better yet, the digestive system of the soul (subconscious). Once revelation is extracted, it births understanding. Knowledge puffs up, but understanding anchors you in truth.

Knowledge lives in the conscious. Once we grind it up by studying, it turns into understanding before making its way into the subconscious (heart). This is to say that knowledge doesn't belong in the control center of the heart (subconscious); understanding belongs there. Wisdom, on the other hand, is a supernatural illumination of that revelation, and it lives in the unconscious. Wisdom is food for our spirit; this is what causes, for example, a believer to praise God unconsciously. Check out this powerful article:

"When he was a chaplain at a nursing home in Chicago, the Rev. James Ellor decided to try an experiment. He found a Sunday school book from the turn of the century, selected the most popular hymns and Bible verses from that time period, and designed a worship service for dementia patients, who had been banned from the chapel after new carpet was installed because of their incontinence. What Ellor discovered has added a new dimension to Alzheimer's treatment: soul care. People with dementia, it turned out, might not be able to recognize their children, but could remember the first verse of beloved hymns from their childhoods, and many could recite Bible verses they had learned when they were younger, like John 3:16 or the Twenty-Third Psalm. Moreover, when given the chance to participate in a modified worship service, they would clap their hands joyfully, and they would often hum hymns and recite Bible verses for several hours after the service ended" (Source: Deseret News/What Alzheimer's disease teaches us about the soul/Jennifer Graham).

This is what King David meant in Psalm 119 when he said, "Thy word have I hid in mine heart, that I might not sin against thee." He also said in Proverbs 2:9-10, "When wisdom entereth into thine heart, and knowledge is pleasant unto thy soul; discretion shall preserve thee, understanding shall keep thee." So again, seasons are time-released capsules of information. If you fill yourself with knowledge, but you don't get understanding, you will become puffed up or, better yet, prideful. If knowledge enters your subconscious, you will become religious. What does this mean? If the information is not digested or broken down, you won't understand it properly, so you'll lean to your own understanding or you will allow others to interpret that information for you. The goal isn't to get a bunch of information. Sure, you should want to pack your head with as much knowledge as possible, but the most important goal if you want to graduate from one season to the next is to get understanding. And remember that wisdom is the principal thing. This means that it's of utmost importance.

Once a season ends, you don't immediately enter the next season. Instead, this is what your migration will look like:

1. **You'll enter into your proverbial Red Sea.** This is the baptism that qualifies you for the next season. This is typically the time when you'll grieve the season that you're leaving behind. This is the moment when the door to Egypt (sin) is still wide open and the way of escape is wide open. This is the point of decision or the proverbial "fork in the road."

2. **Next, you'll enter the wilderness.** This is the hallway between two seasons. This is the bathroom of seasons. During this phase, your goal is to heal and dump out all old and false information that you've acquired in your last season. This is typically the longest part of every believer's process because it is in the wilderness that we discover just how Egyptian (sinful, twisted) we've become. This is when our lusts make their demands and we're

forced to choose between our perversions and our purpose. Sadly enough, most people faint (give up, settle) in the wilderness. Please note that the wilderness is level 5 or, better yet, the bottom of every season. It is the entrance, and this is where you'll find the majority of believers camping out. It's popular to dwell down here because it typically looks, smells and feels like Egypt; the only difference is Pharaoh (the strongman) has lost control over you, however, the habits (strongholds) are very much still in play. That is until you stall and dismantle those systems by repeatedly going against the grain of them to do something new.

3. **Finally, there's the Promised Land of purpose.** But before you enter, you have a few familiar enemies to fight. No, these are not the Egyptians. They are typically family members and people who have begun to feel the ripple effects of your lifestyle change. This is oftentimes when you'll experience one of the most chaotic and difficult challenges—choosing between the people you love the most and your assignment.

Here's what I learned on my journey:

1. The hallway between both seasons is lonely! You're leaving behind the people from your former season, and the people in the seasons up ahead don't trust or like you because of where you've come from. So, you spend quite a bit of time wondering if you've made a huge mistake.

2. Satan loves to catch you in the wilderness by sending wild animals (narcissists and toxic people) after you in the form of romantic interests. Most people are ensnared by these lost souls.

3. You won't understand most of what you experience. Don't quit! Just get yourself a mentor to help you get the language you'll need for the season you're in.

4. And questions—you'll have lots of questions and you may even experience survivor's guilt. This is when you begin to look back and feel guilty for leaving so many loved ones behind, but over the course of time, you'll make peace with your past and come to realize that you didn't leave them behind. They chose to remain where they are, and there was and is nothing you can do about it outside of praying for them. And some of the people you left behind will make you feel guilty for doing so if they get the opportunity to express themselves to you, but don't worry. Chances are, you'll point them in the direction of a church, buy new Bibles for them, talk to them about God, show them a company that's hiring, point them towards a counselor, and you'll soon see that they don't want the information they'll need to move on. They want what's in the hand of God, but they do not want what's in His heart.

5. When you arrive in your Promised Land, you'll be met with the most tangible presence of God that you've ever experienced. Peace, joy and contentment may be foreign to you at this time, so

be prepared to question whether or not what you're feeling is good.

As you navigate through each period and season, just make it a point to not look back. Grieve whenever you need to grieve, pray as much as you can and make sure that you have a therapist, a pastor and a few wise counselors to help you through it all. And finally, don't ever allow yourself to climax until you've reached the pinnacle of your purpose! When this happens, turn around and help others to reach their personal mountaintops as well. You've got this because God's got you!

Your Inner Circle vs. Your Intellectual Circle

One of the ways you can tell that an immature or a toxic person is in your inner circle is when you feel muzzled or afraid to use your voice. In other words, you don't have the freedom to say or post what you want to communicate to the world out of fear that the individual in question will get offended. For example, in the past, I would immediately think of someone who would take offense to what I'd posted or what I was about to post to my Facebook page. This thought would seemingly come out of nowhere, and I'd either hesitate to write the post, publish the post or I'd take it down. Don't get me wrong. You will disagree with those closest to you, and there is nothing wrong with this. After all, you need people to occasionally challenge your perspective! Howbeit, I'm talking about people you've had repeated disagreements with—people whose perspectives don't mirror your own—people who have managed to convince themselves that they need to change your views. This is especially true if their views are more carnal or secular than your own. Maybe they typically engage all of your statuses, but whenever they don't like or comment on your status after an hour or so, you take the status down. This is a sign that you're under control, but it doesn't mean that they are intentionally controlling you. It does mean that something is controlling you, either from within or from without. For example, let's say that you post the following status:

"Ladies, we need to take accountability for the mistakes we make and stop blaming everything on men! Let's not forget that many of us have sons or will have sons someday, and we don't want them to think that they are programmed to fail just because they're males."

This is a great post; right? There's nothing offensive about it; it's a corrective post, and it was written in love. Howbeit, after posting it, your mind is invaded by a series of thoughts. Your best friend, Nancy, is going to take offense to this post because Nancy blames men for everything. You consider taking the post down, but then, you say to yourself, "Let me check her page. Maybe she hasn't been on social media in a few days." So, you open another tab, navigate to Nancy's social media page, and you're horrified to see that she's just posted a status 37 minutes ago. It reads:

"So, my son's father just called and said that he's going to sue me for custody of our son! What a joke! Sometimes, I think men are given one brain cell and they lose it once their first tooth comes in! At this point, I'd be willing to cancel his child support payments for a few months so he can save up his money and buy himself some more brain cells!"

After seeing this post, how do you think you'll feel? You're not going to want to hit the post button on the status you've written because your friend is going to think your status is all about her. But, that's fine. In order to build and maintain relationships, you also need relational sensitivity, so in that moment, you decide to delete the text you were about to post. A few days later, you get another bright idea. You want to post about your big brother's awesome new girlfriend because in the few months that they've been dating, she's pushed him to go back to school, she's taken care of him when he was sick, she's helped him start his window tinting business and she always reaches out to you to see if you need anything. On top of this, she's always praying with you and for you. She's amazing! Overwhelmed by love and appreciation one day, you start writing the post to praise what you hope to be your future sister-in-law, but all of a sudden, you receive a text message from your friend. It reads:

> "Sometimes, I feel like good girls finish last. Do you remember that guy I told you about? We used to flirt everyday when I worked at the dealership. Well, I bumped into him today and he said that he's engaged. And all I've been seeing today on Facebook is one engagement post after another, and one 'in a relationship' status after another. I'm over it."

This seems innocent enough, but you then remember that your friend once had a huge crush on your brother and she absolutely hates his new girlfriend. So, you let out a sigh and you decide to practice relational sensitivity all over again. Two months later, it happens again, but this time, you submit a post that reads:

> "It is summertime right here in Texas, and I can't wait to hit the beach with my new two-piece!"

Again, this is another post with good intentions. Maybe, you've lost a lot of weight and you're proud of your new body. Maybe, you're just excited about the beach. Either way, you haven't done anything wrong in posting this unless your intentions were malicious. Without warning, you receive a call from your friend. "Can we talk?" she asks in an awkwardly low tone. "Sure, what's up?" you ask as you head towards your car. The sound of your friend's breath blowing into the phone's receiver is extremely annoying. She then says, "Listen, we all know that you have a summer body, but you don't have to rub it in everyone's face! Some of us have health conditions that keep us from getting in shape. I came on Facebook looking for some positivity after dealing with a lot of stupidity today, only to come across your insensitive post!" What's happening here is this—you're being controlled. And while the incident with the posts may be innocent enough, the truth is that whenever you have immature people too close to your heart, you will always be reminded of the fact that they are easily offended and super sensitive. What this means is you need new friends! And your old friend needs to move out of your inner circle and into your intellectual circle or out of your life altogether.

What is your inner circle and what is your intellectual circle? Let's revisit the diagram from the first chapter.

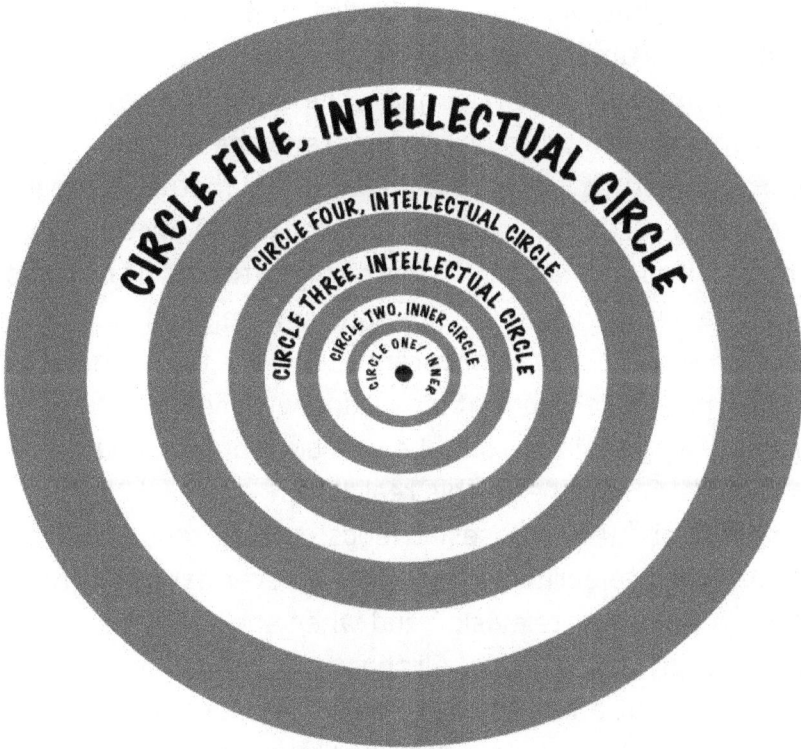

Your heart is the dot in the center of the circle. Remember, the Lord told you to guard it with all diligence. (Note: the word "diligence" is defined by Oxford Languages as "careful and persistent work or effort.") The first two circles are your intimate spaces, and the next three are your intellectual spaces. The majority of the people you will host in your life will enter and remain in your intellectual circle. The people in this particular space will only know surface-level information about you and your life. They may never see you cry, they may never see you in a worried state and they may never see you panic. And if they ever do see you in any of these states, chances are, you will give them surface-level information regarding whatever it is that you're going through. If you give them intimate information, they will automatically enter your intimate circle, and while they may be willing to avail themselves to you when you're in the midst of a storm, the truth is that they may not be mature or healthy enough to occupy that particular space. And once they've entered into this space, it's hard to get them out of it. For example, let's create two characters: Lacey and Felicia. Lacey met Felicia at a conference, and the two women hit it off immediately, but after talking with Felicia a few times, Lacey realized that she was both broken and immature. She came to this realization when Felicia kept gossiping about her closest friends, talking reproachfully about every celebrity pastor that has ever dared to grace the screen of her television and when she spent the night at her boyfriend's house. All the same, Felicia has spoken nonstop about a few of the men who've hurt her. According to her, she's gotten her revenge against two of them, but there was one more ex that she wanted to pay back. Lacey is a minister, but more than that, she truly loves God and is trying to live an intentional life.

One day, Lacey got the news that her great-aunt had just passed away. To make matters worse, she wouldn't be able to attend her funeral because of COVID restrictions. Lacey was heartbroken. She'd spoken with a few members of her family, but the majority of them were unsaved, and the ones that were saved were mostly religious (meaning, they practice the rituals of religion, but didn't necessarily have intimate relationships with God). Lacey even called her best friend, but Nona was on tour with a production company. She'd spoken with Lacey, but she was the main act in a traveling stage play, so she didn't have the time Lacey needed. This is how Felicia crept in. She'd called Lacey after hearing about her great-aunt. At first, Lacey thanked Felicia for her love and support, and she had no intentions of going any deeper into the matter, but something Felicia said triggered a response from her. Felicia said, "Listen, if you need someone to talk to, I'm here for you. I know how hard it can be to grieve. I made the mistake of trying to grieve without any help, and I had to have three years of therapy behind that trauma. When my nephew passed away, I thought my world was coming to an end and I wanted so badly to hear someone say, 'It's okay. He's in a better place,' but Lacey, he wasn't saved. How could he be in a better place?" With those words, Lacey broke. This was exactly what she'd been experiencing! Her great-aunt wasn't saved; she often spoke against religion, but morally, she was a pretty decent woman. Remarkably enough, in that hour, Felicia sounded both mature and understanding, so Lacey began to open up to her. She told Felicia, "I'm scared, I'm mad and I'm confused. I feel like I'm always here for everyone else, but in my hour of need, I don't have anyone to turn to! I've been having trouble sleeping because I keep dreaming about my aunt. No one in the family can help me because they already think I'm crazy simply because I'm saved. And don't mention money! They want all of us to contribute five hundred dollars to my aunt's funeral. As it turns out, she didn't have life insurance. It's a mess!" And just like that, Lacey opened her heart to someone who was supposed to remain in her intellectual space, allowing that person to enter her intimate space. Afterwards, Felicia called Lacey everyday to check on her; she sent her $250 to help with her aunt's funeral and attended the funeral with Lacey. This caused the two ladies to bond, and for about three months, they were inseparable. Lacey even began to distance herself from Nona, pushing her confused friend into her intellectual space, meaning she didn't end their relationship, she simply closed her heart to her, only giving her surface-level information whenever they spoke.

One day, Lacey received a call from her manager, Mrs. Brown. Mrs. Brown informed Lacey that she was no longer allowed to step foot on the company's property. She was terminated because the company had received an anonymous call from a woman claiming that Lacey, who was a supervisor at her job, had clocked in the day of her great-aunt's funeral and then left the premises. She then returned later that day to clock out. This was because the company had refused to give Lacey the day off, saying that her great-aunt did not belong to her immediate family. The anonymous caller also told Mrs. Jones a few horrible things that Lacey had said about her, including the fact that her husband had left her to be with a younger woman, she ate sunflower seeds and spat the shells in the garbage all the time and her oldest son had Tourette Syndrome. According to the caller, Lacey had laughed at the fact that Mrs. Jones hired her son to work in the cafeteria, and whenever they went to lunch, he always insisted on praying over the food. All had always gone well, but Mrs. Jones was always on edge whenever he asked to pray. The supervisor reviewed the video from the day of the funeral and discovered that everything the caller said was true. All the same, Mrs. Jones could also confirm that everything the caller had said about her son, the sunflower seeds and her estranged husband was also true. Lacey was horrified. Who would dare get her fired from a job that she'd had for more than 15 years, and why would they be so cruel?! There was only one answer—Felicia! She was the only person who knew about Lacey clocking in on the day of her great-aunt's funeral, but when Lacey called Felicia to confront her, she did not answer her phone, nor did she respond to Lacey's many text messages.

Three weeks went by and Lacey did not hear from Felicia, nor was she able to reach her. At church one Sunday morning, Lacey had received a message from one of her pastor's armor-bearers. Pastor Lance wanted to see her in his office. Lacey complied. "What's this I hear about you harassing an old friend of yours?" he asked. "And is it true that you lost your job for some questionable behavior? I'm not trying to pry, but as a minister at this church, it is my business how you conduct yourself, because you're not just representing the Kingdom of God, you are also a representative of this ministry." Lacey explained the situation to her pastor before leaving his office in tears. He believed her, but her anger was in the fact that a woman she'd considered to be her friend had betrayed her. What happened here? Simply put, Felicia was not healed, mature or consecrated enough to be in Lacey's intimate space. Believe it or not, as horrible as Felicia may appear to be, she may have been an amazing fixture in Lacey's intellectual space. What Lacey should have done was had a multitude of counselors around her; this way, she wouldn't put the weight of her emotional health on her best friend, Nona. Nona hadn't done anything wrong. She simply wasn't available, and that's okay from time to time. If Lacey had surrounded herself with a multitude of counselors when all had been well in her life, she would have had a few shoulders to cry on. Again, countries don't prepare for war in times of war, they prepare for war in times of peace. In layman's terms, this means that it is better to be proactive than it is to be reactive. Because whenever we're heartbroken, angry or scared, our judgment is clouded. And in those spaces of time, toxic people start sounding relatively mature to us because we are under the influence of pain, fear or frustration. Most of us have experienced this at some point in time or another. We spoke with someone we knew to be toxic, and while they were talking, we inwardly said to ourselves, "She's not that bad after all. She's just misunderstood." And then, we found out later on that the person was as broken or toxic as we'd initially imagined her (or him) to be. This means that you should never move the people around in your intimate/intellectual circle whenever you're in a highly emotional state.

Trust is earned; I think we can all agree with this statement. This means that we shouldn't extend trust to someone we don't know or someone who has proven himself or herself to be unworthy of it. We need to consistently see people in every season of their lives before we extend trust to them. Get this—one of the most surefire signs that someone is a narcissist or a toxic person is:

1. The individual tries to move from the intellectual circle to the intimate circle in a matter of hours, days or weeks, or the person tries to skip the intellectual circle altogether and jump right into your intimate (inner) circle.

2. The person demands, requires or tries to seduce you into trusting him or her, even though the individual in question hasn't earned it.

3. The person begins to target the people in your inner circle, questioning their motives, their authentlclty or their character. For example, your new love interest may say, "Why does your pastor keep talking about money?" In this, he (or she) is trying to plant a negative seed in your heart regarding your pastor. This means that he or she will ultimately seek to drive you away from that pastor, and maybe even away from the church scene altogether.

4. The person gives you intellectual access to himself or herself, but demands to have intimate access to your heart. Sometimes, this demand is verbal, whereas the person will say something along the lines of, "I feel like you don't trust me" or "Why do you have your guards up?" Oftentimes, this demand is nonverbal, whereas the person will ask you questions that are intimate in nature or the person may attempt to gain access to your body, your finances, your material possessions, your home or the people in your intimate circle.

5. The individual pulls away when you don't give him or her intimate access to you (ex: stop calling, call more infrequently, stop sending text messages he or she sends everyday, stop answering your calls, stop responding to your text messages, etc.).

When you're dealing with toxic people and/or narcissists, you will often feel pressured to let down your guards, and one of the ways they'll seduce you into doing this is by giving you intimate details about their lives or by giving you intimate access to certain spaces in their hearts prematurely. They do this because it triggers your need to reciprocate. In other words, we often feel pressured to say to others what they say to us, so if someone says, "You look amazing," we feel obligated to say, "And so do you." If we are sure that the individual will say, "I look a mess," because, for example, her clothes are soiled or her hair is unkempt, we'll find some other way to compliment her. We may say, "You're such a beautiful person" or "Give me that waistline of yours!" All the same, we also feel obligated to give people the level of access to our hearts that they've given us to theirs. For example, if a woman says to you, "I'm almost ashamed to admit this, but I've been trying to stop watching porn," you may feel pressured to share something that is both intimate and embarrassing about your life. For example, a friend of mine told me that she'd met and exchanged numbers with a guy, and two days after meeting him, he'd sent her pictures of his daughters. Of course, this made her feel like she needed to reciprocate by sending him pictures of her children. We talked about it, and I told her about this particular trigger. I told her to be mindful of the guy because, based on what she'd shared with me, he sounded like he was likely narcissistic or toxic. All the same, she falls under the category of people who tend to attract narcissists. Thankfully, she's not desperate to be in a relationship, so she received the warning without incident. Was I telling her to shoo the guy away? No. I simply reminded her to guard her heart, after all, she was experiencing the pressure of this guy trying to enter her intimate space without fully knowing her. This is always a red flag.

Lastly, here are a few facts to consider about your intimate circle:

1. Some of your closest friends will alternate from time to time. For example, someone who has intimate access to you will gradually or sometimes even suddenly move to the intellectual circle because of distance, maturity or offense. Don't always take these moves personally. Like a chess game, God moves people around in your life so that you can grow and you can maximize your fullest potential in any given season. However, if someone distances himself or herself from you in an attempt to punish you, don't allow that person to suddenly reappear in your intimate space. Keep them in your intellectual space, not as a punishment, but because they have proven themselves to be too immature or broken to have intimate access to your heart. Be sure to communicate your new boundaries with them and don't allow them to seduce you into letting them back into your intimate space. If you

feel obligated to let them back in, put them on a probationary period of three to six months. In other words, if they repeat this behavior within that space of time, move them to the proper intellectual circle or out of your life altogether.

2. This is the most coveted position in your life; don't freely or easily give people access to this space. Healthy people will be patient and they'll prove themselves to be worthy of whatever circle you give them access to over time. All the same, you will prove yourself worthy of whatever access they give you.

3. People who display symptoms of jealousy and immaturity should never have intimate access to you, otherwise, you will experience a lot of unnecessary warfare. They may be good people, but good people can do bad things. Don't always look for good people, look for growing people.

Next, let's talk about your intellectual circle. Think of the three levels of your intellectual circle as layers of ground. The people on the surface or, better yet, Circle 5 are people you associate with. They may be kind and they may be good and Godly people, but they may be in Circle 5 because:

1. Neither of you has ever made any attempt to get to know one another better or you simply may be too busy to bond.

2. They may be relatively immature. Please note that immature people aren't necessarily bad people, but

they can do hurtful things or become bad influences if allowed too close.

3. They may be toxic, but for some reason, you feel obligated to give them some measure of access to your life.

4. They may be new to your life. Everyone should start in Circle 5 and move their way up. You should never place someone you barely know, for example, in Circle 3 just because you had a great conversation with them, you can relate to them in so many ways or because they helped you in one way or another.

5. They are affiliated with someone who doesn't care too much for you, and while they may have never done anything wrong to you, their association with an enemy of yours makes them a high risk.

With these people, you give them surface-level information, meaning, you only share with them what can be clearly seen by the people around you. For example, let's say that someone asked me, "Hey, how are you? How was your day? What did you do today?" Imagine that I've had a not-so-great day. For example, let's say that I lost my job today. Look at the chart below to gauge my response to each circle.

Circle	My Answer
5	Hi! I'm blessed! I can't complain. Just work and home; that's all. How about you?
4	Hi! I'm blessed! No sense in complaining, after all, it's nothing that God can't handle; right? How about you?

Circle	My Answer
3	Hey girl! I'm good. How are you? I'm not going to lie, I lost my job today because someone decided to lie on me. If you know someone who's hiring, please let me know and put in a good word for me.
2	Hey sis! Things could be better. I lost my job today because one of my co-workers decided to lie on me. Can you believe that? I work for (Name the Company, Incorporated) as an operator and the girl told my boss that I'd yelled at a customer. Anyhow, I filed an appeal, so definitely keep me in your prayers. And if you know someone who's hiring, please let me know.
1	Hey sis! I'm not doing so well. I just lost my job today because my co-worker lied on me. Do you remember that girl named Sally that I told you about? Yeah, so she told my boss that I yelled at a customer today, and this was simply not true. Of course, my boss didn't question her. I think it has a lot to do with that time I caught them holding hands in the elevator. I don't know what to do. Please pray for me.

Notice the different approaches I took to answer that question. This is why it is important to take a moment to consider the question that was asked, and then consider where the person who posed the question falls in your life. In other words, don't answer emotionally.

- **Circle 5:** You'll notice that with someone in Circle 5, I didn't give her any indication that something was wrong. And to keep her from prying, I asked her, "How about you?" By doing this, I shifted the conversation.

- **Circle 4:** My choice of words indicates that something could potentially be challenging me, but I didn't give any other information, and if she tries to dig into the situation, I'll give her a little insight before bringing her back to the surface-level with something along the lines of, "No, all is well. Just a few challenges in the workplace. Just keep me lifted in prayer. How's your mom doing?" Notice that I keep shifting the conversation away from me and back to her? All the same, the comment about the workplace is something I'd say if the person is Christian and I believe that she can get a prayer through to God. Other than that, I would keep the conversation just above the surface.

- **Circle 3:** This person has a measure of trust, even though he or she is in the intellectual circle. Notice that I gave her (let's pretend it's a woman) just enough information to know what's going on in my life, without giving her the who's who of my problems. I won't necessarily tell her where I work, the names of the people involved or just what the accusation was. Why? Chances are, I don't know who she's connected to because we're not that close, and I don't know what she will do with that information. Nevertheless, I trust her enough to maybe encourage me, pray for me and maybe even check in on me from time to time.

- **Circle 2:** This person is in my inner circle, also known as my intimate circle, so I trust her (or him) with a lot of the details. I won't be as open with this individual as I would be with someone who's in Circle 1, only because this person may be a friend, and not necessarily a close friend or a best friend. So, while I may share a lot of the details with her, I won't necessarily give up any names unless I believe that doing so would help my cause.

- **Circle 1:** Notice that with this particular friend, I'm incredibly detailed. I've told her what I've just experienced and why I believe I experienced it. Why am I sharing the intimate details with her? Because I have theories surrounding why I was terminated, and whenever we have theories, we will bounce them off of someone because we want more insight. All the same, these details could easily turn to gossip if I shared them with the wrong person. It's not gossip because I saw them holding hands; gossip is information and assumptions that has not been proven to be true, however, if I share these details with, for example, a co-worker, it could easily set the stage for gossip and rumors. All the same, in order for someone to be this close to me, I would know that the person isn't a gossiper and that the person will hold me accountable for the words I speak and the role I played in my own termination.

Keep in mind that some of these people are moving away from your heart, meaning, you've moved them from one circle to another because they have proven themselves to be immature or somewhat toxic. In other words, use wisdom when sharing key information with people. All the same, some people are migrating closer to your heart, but your objective should never be to take someone from, for example, Circle 3 to Circle 1. Your objective should always be to see where everyone fits and functions best in your life. So, if someone in Circle 3 proves themselves to be mature enough and healthy enough to enter into your intimate circle, the next stop for them is Circle 2, and you have to leave them there until you have examined their fruit over the course of time to see if that space is a good fit for them.

I know this may sound complicated at first, but over the course of time, it will become second nature to you, and you will discover just how good and peaceful your life is when everyone in your life is in their rightful places. All the same, your discernment will grow majorly because you will come to better understand the signs and symptoms of Narcissistic Personality Disorder and every other toxic trait that broken people tend to exhibit. Your intellectual circle is designed for you to exchange information with people, after all, we were formed by the Word, and we were created in His image. This means that we are words of God, while Jesus is the Word of God. As words, every time we connect ourselves with other people, we form sentences, paragraphs and stories. If the story is filled with drama, broken hearts and sinful behaviors, we have the wrong people in our lives, or we have the right people in the wrong spaces. Think of it this way—if you had a two-year old in your house, chances are, the child belongs there, even though the child is immature. Nevertheless, you would not give that child access to anything valuable or dangerous. For example, the child wouldn't have access to any weapons that he (let's pretend the child is a male) could use to harm himself or anyone else, nor would the child have access to a vault filled with valuables. All the same, you'd place any and everything that's fragile high enough so the child couldn't reach it. Then again, for the things that you have to keep low, you'd teach the child not to touch. The goal isn't to get rid of the child because he's a child; the goal is to make sure that your home is child-proof. Utilize that same concept or strategy with people. The objective isn't to discard every broken or immature person in your life. The goal is to only give them roles and responsibilities that they are mature enough to handle.

Notice that the intimate circle is small and the intellectual circles gets bigger and bigger as it moves away from your heart. Howbeit, any time we place people in the wrong spaces and circles, offense, hurt and trauma are all inevitable. While there are evil people in the world, not everyone is as evil as we make them out to be. Some people are simply too immature to occupy the roles that we want them to serve in, and this is not always a reflection of their character. Sometimes, it's a reflection of our own brokenness and need for validation. Sometimes, we have voids that we want to silence, so we give people spaces and places in our hearts that they are not wise enough to fill. We then play the victim when they prove themselves to be incapable of illuminating the darkness of our voids. Understand this—the Bible says that there is safety in the multitude of counselors (see Proverbs 11:14). This means that it's dangerous to be without them.

How do you get a multitude of counselors?
1. Pray and ask the Lord to send them.
2. Before He sends them, commit to honoring them. Don't be easily offended or offensive. Don't try to force your beliefs or preferences upon them.
3. Allow your mentors and other leaders into your intimate circle if you want help with the intimate details of your life, but never try to get into their intimate circles because doing so would only set the stage for familiarity. How dangerous is familiarity? In truth, most people think they can handle it and are offended at the thought of not being able to access the intimate details of their leaders' lives, but the moment they do get access, they become offensive. Again, this is called the Grenade Effect.
4. Position yourself to receive wise counsel. One of the best ways to do this is to volunteer at your church.
5. Follow through with honoring them. For example, don't ask someone to lunch just so you can pick that person's brain, and then turn around and ask for two tickets, or worse, expect them to pay your tab. Always try to out-bless the person who's blessing you.
6. Listen to wise counsel, even when you don't like what's being shared with you.

7. If you get, for example, three conflicting pieces of advice, God wants you to turn to Him. Pray and wait on Him. Do not accept the advice that you favor, and then claim that it was God that told you to do so! In other words, never lie to God.

8. Don't overdo it! Sometimes, people utilize their counselors for every single issue, and this can cause the other person to feel burnt out. Don't invade the person's life. Just text and ask them if they're available, rather than calling them out of the blue. Also, be sure to let them know when all is well, and again, don't expect them to fix every issue in your life. Always be considerate; this is the highest form of appreciation.

Remember, you got this because God's got you! Pray about everything and everyone! It is the will of God that you prosper and that your days are filled with joy, peace and laughter. It is the will of God that you thrive in every area of your life. It is the will of God that all of your voids are filled with His presence and that you are made whole! It is the will of God that you become everything He's designed you to be! Keep pushing; don't quit and don't get comfortable in the wrong realm! Make fear afraid of you!

Embracing the Renewed You

In order to receive deliverance from old mindsets and systems, you have to go low! In other words, you have to humble yourself.

- **Matthew 23:12:** And whosoever shall exalt himself shall be abased; and he that shall humble himself shall be exalted.
- **James 4:10:** Humble yourselves in the sight of the Lord, and he shall lift you up.
- **1 Peter 5:6:** Humble yourselves therefore under the mighty hand of God, that he may exalt you in due time.

The Israelites found themselves in the greatest battle of their lives. This battle was far worse than the warfare they'd experienced after Pharaoh ordered the Egyptians to toss all of their infant boys into the Nile River; this was after his failed attempt to get the midwives to assassinate the young boys (see Exodus 1:15-22). The Israelites found themselves caught between a sea and an angry mob of soldiers desperate to bring them back into captivity. And just as the pressure was about to reach its peak, Moses suddenly lifted up his staff and the Red Sea opened. The Israelites could not believe their eyes, but they didn't have time to marvel at the miracle. They had to either rush into the depths of the Sea—the very sea that held the lifeless bodies of the young boys who had been killed some 80 years prior at Pharaoh's command—or they had to risk being killed, and the ones who weren't killed would have likely been beaten and brought back into captivity, only to have their burdens made heavier. And get this—the Israelites didn't just step on dry ground. They had to go low or descend into the depths of the sea to get their deliverance; this represents baptism. Historians believe that the Israelites crossed the Red Sea through the Gulf of Aqaba, which today is about 500 meters in depth; that's over 1600 feet! All the same, you have to humble yourself to escape a season. Remember, a season is a mindset that locks you into a space of time called a realm. Your realm is your reality. Each realm has a certain measure of revelation (revealed information). Once you have taken all that you are supposed to take from a particular realm, your assignment is to graduate to the next realm. As a reminder, if you don't escape a season when God opens the door for you to do so, you will become a master manipulator. This doesn't necessarily mean that you'll become evil and start intentionally hurting people. What it means is that you'll go into survival mode, and this will cause you to voluntarily or involuntarily compete with and hurt people. In other words, you will become one of the archetypal "crabs in a bucket." When you graduate from one realm to the other, you go from being the teacher and an expert in the realm you've exited to being a student in the next realm. Think of it this way—in a middle school, the eighth graders are the seniors at their schools, but once they leave middle school and enter high school, they then become the juniors. Imagine a student refusing to leave the eighth grade simply because he loves the attention he gets from the sixth and seventh graders. More than likely, that kid would become a bully; right? This is because he would be intoxicated with power and intimidated by anyone who dared to dream bigger than himself. Nevertheless, if he wants to ascend, he has to be willing to humble himself and become a freshman again.

All the same, the Israelites had burned their bridges with the Egyptians. They'd taken gold from the people, plus, they were now feared and despised by the people. One of the lessons to take from this is—whenever God brings you out of a season, He will oftentimes cause you to burn the bridges that would allow you to return to that season; this way, you can never return to the ditches that He has delivered you from. For example, once the Egyptians crossed over the Red Sea, the Lord caused the sea to go back into place, covering up the dry ground. Please note that by burning bridges, I don't mean that you have to mistreat, dishonor or ridicule the people. As a matter of fact, you have to honor your way out of a season. Nevertheless, by burning bridges, I mean that you should not leave any doors cracked or allow anyone to reserve you a seat in the realm that you are coming out of. A better way to say this is—you have to finalize your dealings with people and realities by:
1. Changing your mind.
2. Setting boundaries and solidifying them.
3. Growing up (maturation).

Before their deliverance was complete, the Israelites stepped into the midst of the Red Sea. Their hearts were racing, their adrenaline was at its peak and their stomachs were in knots. They could hear the yells of the Egyptian army gaining up on them; they could hear the sounds of the water around them under pressure, and they could hear the voices of terror coming from amongst them. Nevertheless, they kept crossing the sea until they reached the desert of Shur. Another lesson to take from this is—when God takes you from one season, He takes you into the hallway of your next season; this hallway starts with a desert or a dry place. It is in this space that you will deal with the greatest temptation to return to the bondage that God has delivered you from. Don't turn back or look back; you have to trust in the Lord, and once you come out of that part of the hallway, you will enter the second level of the hallway; this is the wilderness. The wilderness is not a place to date or build a family! It's a time to move forward; to heal, to reflect, to forgive and to plan for the future. This is the longest and most treacherous part of our journeys because we have to unlearn what we once learned in Egypt (sin) before learning the language of the Kingdom. We do this, of course, by studying and applying the Word of God daily.

The third and most intense level of warfare takes place right when you're about to enter your personal Promised Land; this is the place where you'll find most of your answered prayers, especially the ones that are major to you. So, it would only make sense that Satan attacks you with everything he has before you enter into this section of your journey. This is because:

1. He feels entitled to your soul.

2. He feels entitled to your children.
3. He knows that your testimony will help to free others.

What is the purpose of warfare? In the midst of his own fiery battle, Job answered this question for us. "But He knoweth the way that I take; when He hath tried me, I shall come forth as gold" (Job 23:10). Why gold? Here are a few facts about gold that may interest you:

Gold is extremely ductile. A single ounce of gold can be stretched into a gold thread 5 miles long.
Gold is the most non-reactive of all metals and does not rust.
Gold can conduct heat and electricity.
Gold is chemically inactive and is not affected by air, heat or moisture.
Pure Gold is so soft that it can be molded by hand.
Source: UK Bullion: Investments for Tomorrow/30 Facts About Gold That You May Not Know.

Notice the last pointer—pure gold is so soft or pliable that it can be molded by hand. Isaiah 64:8 reads, "But now, O LORD, thou art our father; we are the clay, and thou our potter; and we all are the work of thy hand." Additionally, consider the prophet Jeremiah's encounter with a potter, and the Word of the Lord that followed. Jeremiah 18:1-6 reads, "The word which came to Jeremiah from the LORD, saying, Arise, and go down to the potter's house, and there I will cause thee to hear my words. Then I went down to the potter's house, and, behold, he wrought a work on the wheels. And the vessel that he made of clay was marred in the hand of the potter: so he made it again another vessel, as seemed good to the potter to make it. Then the word of the LORD came to me, saying, O house of Israel, cannot I do with you as this potter? Saith the LORD. Behold, as the clay is in the potter's hand, so are ye in mine hand, O house of Israel." In other words, you are in God's hands.

- He formed you.
- Sin deformed you.
- And now, you're being transformed by the renewing of your mind.

How does God transform us? Through information, of course. Jesus is the Word of God; you and I are words of God. We are an embodiment of words that we've spoken, words that others have spoken over us, words that others have spoken about us, words that we've studied and accepted, words that we've heard and believed—each one of us is a body of words. Whenever we embody what God said about us and release every other word, we begin to flow without opposition. Nevertheless, most of us are a combination of words that are warring against one another. Sure, we know that we're healed, but we may find ourselves struggling with whatever reports our doctors have given us. Sure, we know that we are the head and not the tail, however, we may still struggle with walking in the authority that Jesus has afforded us. And yes, we are more than conquerors in Christ, but there are days when we feel, act and reason as victims. This is because we may know the scriptures, but somehow, another set of words has entered into our systems and began to battle with the Word of God. And whatever we believe, we become. This is why we have to meditate on the Word of God daily; this way, we can cast down every other word that dares to exalt itself against the knowledge of God, and bring every thought into captivity to the obedience of Christ (see 2 Corinthians 10:5); this way, like gold, you can:

1. Be stretched beyond your limitations. In other words, you can tap into the supernatural realm.
2. You won't be reactive (emotional; fearful) to the enemy's lies. Instead, you will stand your ground in faith.
3. You will be able to conduct heat and electricity or, better yet, you will be a conduit of power that God can express Himself through.
4. You won't be affected by the weather of whatever season you're in, or the people around you. You will be steadfast, unmovable and always abounding in the work of the Lord.
5. God can readily and easily transform you without you having to be broken first. Please note that clay, once it's been exposed to air, hardens. In order for that clay to be transformed, it has to be broken and soaked in water. This allows it to be malleable, but unlike hard clay or a stubborn soul, you will yield yourself to God because your trust for Him will be nothing short of supernatural.

A renewed mind qualifies you for the favor and blessings of God. This includes whatever you've been praying about that, of course, is within the confines of His will. Let the

Lord surround you with the right people, and remember this—don't be afraid to lose the wrong ones. Here are a few truths and reminders for you to apply on your new journey:

1. Think as a Producer, and not as a Consumer. Always produce more than you consume, and always consume less than you produce.

2. Be honest with yourself. If you have people in your intimate circle who should be in your intellectual circle, you don't have to write them a bunch of "dear John" letters. You simply need to change your mind and set boundaries. They will either fall into place or fall away.

3. The greatest enemy of the gifted is comfort. Don't allow yourself to get too comfortable in any given season. Always take yourself out of your comfort zone so that anytime you are thrust out of it, you won't end up suffering through trauma and having to heal from the event.

4. Your voids are hungry! Don't toss people at your voids, toss information at them! Mainly, toss the Word of God at them.

5. Take accountability for every wrong you've somehow overlooked; this way, you can complete the circle of every given season and move on to your next season.

6. Forgive others by reminding yourself that they were and maybe still are broken; then again, always find your error or mistake in everything that happened to the adult-sized you.

7. Stop trying to be normal. The world keeps changing

their definition of "normal" every single day, and nowadays, what the world considers to be normal is demonized, mentally deranged people who are crazy enough to challenge God.

8. Heal so the human scabs (narcissists and toxic people) can fall away from you.
9. Study and show yourself approved for the next level.
10. Get yourself a few counselors, but be sure to pray about them first! There is safety in the multitude of counselors.

And the main thing is—be intentional. In other words, do everything on purpose, understanding that everything that you do will create a domino effect called reaping. In other words, sow what you want to reap, and uproot everything that works against God's plan for your life. Additionally, always seek to grow in your relational acumen to ensure that all of your soldiers and players are in place; this way, you can focus on doing what God created you to do. Simply put, don't give place to the enemy!

www.ingramcontent.com/pod-product-compliance
Lightning Source LLC
Chambersburg PA
CBHW072343090426
42741CB00012B/2899